VIVAT! VIVAT REGINA!

Robert Bolt sees Mary Queen of Scots and her cousin Elizabeth I as figures on a seesaw, so similar and opposite. They were enemies, but mutually fascinated. 'I found their individual stories merely sad,' he writes in his Introduction to the play. 'But when I put the two together a theme seemed to emerge with uncanny clarity, as though they had been put on earth to illustrate it. The theme is Power, the pressures and penalties of Power, the gap between the fine appearance which Power makes and the shameful shifts by which it is sustained. And above all the unnaturalness of Power, the impermissible sacrifice of self which Power demands, and gets, and squanders; to what purpose?'

The clash between two remarkable women and heads of states is here presented as essential drama for the modern theatre, with all its resources of fluency, flexibility and imaginative stimulus.

32m 4f.

THE HEREFORD PLAYS

General Editor: E. R. Wood

Robert Bolt

Vivat! Vivat Regina!

Introduction by
THE AUTHOR

with Commentary and Notes by
E. R. WOOD

HEINEMANN EDUCATIONAL BOOKS
LONDON

Heinemann Educational Books Ltd

LONDON   EDINBURGH   MELBOURNE   AUCKLAND   TORONTO
HONG KONG   SINGAPORE   KUALA LUMPUR
IBADAN   NAIROBI   JOHANNESBURG
LUSAKA   NEW DELHI

ISBN 0 435 22104 3

Published by
Heinemann Educational Books Ltd
48 Charles Street, London W1X 8AH
Printed in Great Britain by
William Clowes & Sons Limited
London, Colchester and Beccles

CONTENTS

INTRODUCTION

The writer of an historical play is a kind of playwright, not a kind of historian. But I think he is obliged to be as accurate, historically, as he can.

He has borrowed not only his story but some of his emotion from actual people who actually lived. He is in debt to them for their virtues and vices, imaginatively energized by the actual energy they expended. He owes them the truth and is a kind of crook if he doesn't pay up.

Then too, the audience brings a special credulity to a history play. They credit the events they see enacted with a degree of actuality not claimed for events—like Shylock's bargain—which are purely theatrical. We are additionally moved when an actor plays out the noble death of an historical character by the knowledge that some such person did make some such death. And the playwright exploits this. Because everybody in the audience knows that Joan of Arc really was executed the playwright can take her to her death with an authority and an appearance of inevitability which he would otherwise have to work for. He can only honour this double debt to his characters and to his audience by sticking to the facts.

To what extent is this a restriction, an abdication from creative freedom and responsibility?

Well in the first place, historical facts are imperfectly known, even important facts about important people. On the evidence available we cannot know for certain (though few historians doubt it) that it really was Bothwell who murdered Darnley, or whether Mary married Bothwell willingly or was abducted. Still less, on the evidence available, can we know what it was that kept Elizabeth unmarried to the end.

The playwright does not bind himself to anything constructed of cast-iron when he binds himself to history.

Of course I couldn't write a play in which Mary Stuart was a virgin and Bothwell ran off with Elizabeth and claim it was historical. There are limits.

But if the playwright finds the limits limiting then he is writing the wrong play. If he is rightly in love with his subject then the facts—even those which do not fit his preconceptions or which fit least readily upon a stage—will present themselves as opportunity and stimulus, not limitation.

More properly it is not his subject which the playwright loves but the play he hopes to write about it. More properly yet the playwright has a latent love for the play *form*, which he hopes will crystallize about his subject; he has in his heart a play-shaped vacancy which he will fill now with his subject.

The filling process will be strenuous. The subject, though it is not cast-iron, yet it does have a shape of its own. And the play form though it is flexible yet it does have limits too—my goodness has it not! But so has every form. Painters at their work will curse the disabilities of paint. But it is only because of what paint will not do that it can be got to do what it sometimes marvellously will. If paint could do everything then only God could work with it and paint would be the substance of the Universe instead of what it is, an artist's material. All forms of art derive their power from their limits and the artist finds it so.

That is not to say that he finds it agreeable. I cursed plentifully as I cast about for ways to accommodate the facts about Elizabeth and Mary in the form of a two act play.

The most obvious problem was that of sheer length. I was to collapse the events of twenty years into three hours.

The next difficulty was that my two protagonists never met. Schiller in his play invents a 'secret' meeting in Fotheringay Park. But the fact is that the two never came within a hundred miles of one another.

And then their two stories were so different. Mary plunged to final disaster by a pell mell succession of passionate actions, by expense. Elizabeth rose cautiously to her final triumph, by accumulation, mistrusting action.

I found their individual stories merely sad. But when I put the two together a theme seemed to emerge with uncanny clarity, as though they had been put on earth to illustrate it. The theme is Power, the pressures and the penalties of Power, the gap between the fine appearance which Power makes and the shameful shifts by which it is sustained. Above all the unnaturalness of Power, the impermissible sacrifice of self which Power demands, and gets, and squanders; to what purpose?

Elizabeth, a legendary political virtuose ('She alone knows how to rule!' exclaimed the cynical Henry of Navarre in a rare moment of enthusiasm) lived to be old; and hideous; and so neurotically deprived that all her courtiers, greybeards and boys, had to go through the motions of being in love with her.

Mary was a legendary femme fatale. Her portraits do not show by our standards a beauty but her contemporaries, friends and enemies alike, agree that she was irresistible. 'The finest she that ever was' reported one hostile emissary to Scotland. And another, reeling from an early interview: 'What a princess, what a lady!' The young French courtier-poet Chastelard from the death cell (where he had been sent for hiding in her bedroom) wrote: 'La plus belle, et la plus cruelle . . .' Yet the brilliant creature, once Queen of two countries—some thought three— died alone and in prison, unwanted and helpless.

They are figures on a see-saw, so similar and opposite. They were enemies but mutually fascinated. Each wore the other's portrait in a locket.

Elizabeth wanted to marry only one man in her life, the dashing Robert Dudley. But Robert Dudley fell under suspicion of murdering his wife. For Queen Elizabeth the mere suspicion was enough to prevent the marriage. Bothwell really did murder Mary's husband, yet Mary married him, and ceased to be a Queen in consequence.

Then when Elizabeth gave up Dudley, she offered him to Mary. It would have been a good political stroke, but surely there is something psychologically odd about it? Mary thought so, for she flew into a rage which shook the walls of Holy-rood.

And finally, long after Mary had been executed by Elizabeth's command, Elizabeth herself lay dying. She wouldn't go to bed but lay on cushions day and night. Her bed would be her death-bed and she was not prepared to die. Did she feel she had not lived? Her one remaining duty was to name who should succeed her. And she, who had never failed her duty, couldn't bring herself to do it. At length Robert Cecil plucked up courage and whispered a name in her ear. She nodded, and died. The name was that of James Stuart, Mary Stuart's child.

It is all almost too felicitous dramatically, and I find it terribly moving as well.

To make one story of the two I had to adopt a form of play which could leap across both miles and months without a break, without a change of set; an overtly theatrical, highly artificial form. I happen to like that kind of play and no doubt was attracted to this subject by an intimation that some such form would be required.

I got so cavalier with miles and months at last that I put Mary and Elizabeth on stage together though the one remained in Scotland and the other in London. At Mary's crisis I brought Spain and Italy on stage as well and represented some months of critical diplomacy in a minute's interchange between the assembled potentates, presided over by John Knox with the Edinburgh mob as chorus in the wings. The stage at that juncture is no actual place, the minute that passes is not actual time; it is theatre merely.

By a more moderate distillation in the same convention I hoped to present the confused eventfulness of Mary's life as a series of single theatrical happenings, and to present the tortuous complexities of Elizabeth's policy as an immediate response. I hoped, that is, that the two would pass a single narrative one to the other as relay runners exchange the baton. The point I am trying to make is this: that as a playwright I found the form exciting, and it was forced upon me by the historical facts.

I found the form exciting because I think that Theatre should be, not larger than life—I don't think anything can be that—but more significant than life, or rather—since nothing can be that either—should reveal the significance that is in life, proclaim that life does have significance.

There are plays I know, say Chekhov's, which drily demonstrate that life as we live it has little significance. But implicit in such plays is an invitation to live otherwise, an implication that we are letting life down. And there are plays (perhaps the best of our modern plays) which bitterly affirm that life *in its essence* has no significance. But the value of these plays is, as it seems to me, their bitterness. A Beckett character does not merely deny the existence of God: he upbraids God (*le salaud*) for not existing. The implication is that God ought to exist, that life ought to have significance, is intolerable without it. And the start and conclusion of such plays is the existential determination to impose significance on life or penetrate life with significance, by an act of the human will.

Indeed, I can't see why a man who really believed (that is, believed and accepted) that life has and can have no significance should do anything at all, unless to end it. But write a play is the last thing he would do.

For there is something about Theatre—the framing of the action on the stage, the compression of the action in a little time, the bright lighting of the action, the knowledge of the audience that the action is predetermined (as it were artificially fated)—which compels the characters to be or seem significant. The most subtle analysis of life is perhaps to be found in the novel, the most lyric celebration of it perhaps in verse; but the giant exemplars of living (like Lear and Oedipus) are to be found on stage. It is no accident that Freud should name the springs of action after characters from Greek drama. And Shakespeare has the Prince of Denmark find himself inadequate by measurement against a Player King because the play's the thing which isolates and demonstrates whatever is significant in life. If nothing in life truly is significant then truly the best that Theatre can do is destroy itself and come to an end, in anti-theatre.

I am pro-Theatre. I believe that even now life does somehow have significance and I believe that Theatre is well-adapted to affirm significance and not well-adapted to deny it.

Certainly, in life as we live it our significance is not very obvious. Most of our lives we merely pass. It is only at moments of crisis that we think (and maybe speak and act) significantly. No, the crisis of action, the hard and consequential choice which forces a man to appraise himself and reveals his nature, is really rather rare. Most crises as we all know are seemingly causeless inner crises which pass unnoticed by any but ourselves, avoided or met, leaving our natures enhanced or diminished.

It indicates the nature of Theatre, what Theatre is good for and what not, that on the stage as not in life an inner crisis must have a cause which can be seen and issue in an adequate effect, or it will merely be bewildering. This is T. S. Eliot's famous 'objective correlation', the correlation between state of mind and action, the lack of which in Hamlet led Eliot to judge *Hamlet* finally unsatisfactory.

Now if in real life it is only rarely and fleetingly that we become aware of life's significance and if theatrical characters must be continuously and expressively aware of it, then the playwright is to put people on the stage as they are not in real life. And yet the audience must in some sense believe in them.

How am I to help my audience to this belief—or 'willing suspension of disbelief'? The obvious thing would seem to be to close the gap between the stage and life by having the stage imitate life as closely as possible. Beerbohm Tree put real live rabbits in Titania's wood. Alas, they stopped the show, which could not proceed until these furry atoms of real life had been chased from the stage; where they had no place. It was not merely that their authentic little presences underlined the artificiality of Titania's cardboard trees; they underlined the artificiality of the whole theatrical enterprise, the words and actions of the actors too. To invite direct comparison with life is theatrical suicide.

Of course the rabbits are a bit extreme, and Titania and the others were to speak not natural speech but Shakespearean speeches. If the setting were less ambitious (a contemporary drawing-room say, instead of an Athenian wood) and the actors spoke less splendidly, might it not be possible to reproduce real life on stage? This is the 'fourth wall' drama, in which the proscenium arch is treated as a glass wall of the room where the actors are supposedly living out the action, unaware of the audience. Actors and set-designers of this school attain an extraordinary skill in reproducing the details of real life. But it remains a skill. The narrow limits of the stage continue to obtrude—those wings and drapes and changing lights are visible however cleverly disguised, those off-stage sound effects however like the real thing are obstinately sound-effects, off-stage; the comings and goings of the characters however nonchalantly executed remain entrances and exits ingeniously contrived by the dramatist so that the drama may unfold all in that one room. And if it is a drama, it is not the 'slice of life' which fourth wall drama aimed to be. If the play is to be a slice of life it must bear a one-to-one correlation to life, and the bulk of it must be undramatic. And an undramatic drama is nothing.

By dramatic I don't mean melodramatic. Chekhov is dramatic. But it is true that slice of life drama finds it more difficult to be dramatic than openly artificial drama. Playwrights of the school draw in their horns; instead of Kings and Princes in passionate conflict issuing in murders, they dealt in family misunderstandings issuing in an engagement or a bankruptcy. And actors of the school eschewed artificial eloquence of word and gesture and studied the stumblings of real life words and gestures. But stumblings which are studied are artificial stumblings, and latterly the most sincere and earnest actors of this school have brought genuine stumblings on stage, they have improvised, each night a new spontaneous performance sometimes with new words. This ought to give each night's performance a peculiar truth and freshness. But it doesn't. Wholehearted spontaneity is impossible on stage. Does the actor turn up at the theatre for each performance on spontaneous impulse every night? Is it his spontaneous wish each night to perform the part assigned to him and not another? Does he exit and enter as required by the other actors, spontaneously? It is a very compromised spontaneity. And compromised spontaneity is disagreeable. Personally, I find 'spontaneous' behaviour on the stage as uncomfortable as theatrical behaviour in real life. Both are false. Your rabbits are your only genuine improvisers.

The desire of these actors to be genuine is, and historically was, a good reaction away from bombast, but the only way for an actor to be genuine is to accept that he is acting and be openly artificial. All these attempts to close the gap between the stage and real life by pretending that it isn't there are doomed, and widen it. The gap must be accepted and, I believe, exploited.

Because there is this gap a play is not a slice of life; it is a metaphor for life. In any metaphor there must be a likeness between the things compared or the comparison won't hold. But there must be unlikeness too or the comparison will not illuminate. To compare a leather-bound book to a box is fair enough but tells us little; the two things are too similar. To describe a Greek vase as the bride of quietness tells us much; it takes a poet to point out the similarity between a young woman and an ancient pot—though once he has done it we shall look at both with a different eye. In the same way, King Lear and Oedipus are not very much like people in real life. Such speech and deed in real life would be dotty. But on the stage where they belong they tell us much about real life, enhance it for us, proclaim and seem to prove, while the performance lasts, that life, though tragic, has significance and is worth living.

So Theatre must be both like and unlike real life, people in plays both like and unlike real people. One solution (not *the* solution but one solution) is to set the action in a real world but a world well removed from our own. Shakespeare never set a play in Elizabethan London. He put his people in the past or in some never-never land like Venice or Illyria. Today when everyone has some idea what life is like in distant places, distance of time is more effective.

History is Dutch courage for the dramatist and for the audience both a pledge of actuality and a release from it. From men in cloaks and feathered hats we can accept a continuously high pitch of speech and action not because we seriously think they really did continuously speak and act like that but because we don't know how they spoke and only know the more dramatic of their actions. If I think of my next-door neighbour, I see a rumpled thing all blurred and merged into a wilderness of circumstances. If I think of Walter Raleigh I see a vivid figure floating free and capable of anything. It wasn't so of course. His life was just as bogged down in domestic detail as my neighbour's, and my own; but since my ignorance has freed him from domestic detail he will be as much at home on stage as any other place. The few things we do know of him are sufficiently dramatic in all conscience. And that's another thing.

The people that we know about from history tend to be important people, like Kings and Queens. Now I don't think that the life of a Queen is *ex-officio* any more significant, has any more value, than the life of an ordinary person. Her actions have more consequences yes, but what consequences? Consequences, finally, for the lives of ordinary people. So the seeming significance which she derives from her office derives from the significance of ordinary people, and can't be more. Whatever significance she has, she has as a woman. She may be a great woman, a great soul with more significance than most of us, but she might have been that in any station. A woman dying old and lonely is just that. It does not alter her predicament that she is splendidly dressed and may give orders and be obeyed.

But it does throw her predicament—the predicament of any such old woman—into theatrical relief. She who plays the Queen may enter from nowhere along a red carpet to a fanfare of trumpets and express her predicament in speech of such magnificence and accuracy as no real woman ever spoke, yet cause the audience no discomfort. She who plays the wife of a suburban grocer must come in from the bus-stop, hang up her raincoat, and express herself as eloquently as is plausible. Small wonder that so many realistic plays have centred on our failure to communicate. The fanfare and the carpet are theatrical devices, with an historical excuse.

Shakespeare's people spoke blank verse, which no real people ever did, in ancient Rome no more than in Elizabethan London. It is the language of Theatre only. He sets his play in Rome not London to avoid an irrelevant comparison between his speeches and real speech. He wants his unreal speech to be accepted.

And he wants it accepted in all its unreality, as actual theatre, not imitation life. He underlines its unreality by slipping in colloquial scenes replete with Elizabethan slang. He emphasizes that the actor is not really Julius Caesar by giving him a chiming clock; Macbeth's Porter comments on Elizabethan politics; Lear's Fool on Tudor local government; deliberate anachronisms to remind his audience that the gap between themselves and the characters is not historical but theatrical. To keep his audience he must still provide good theatre; but it will be good or bad by theatre's laws, not the laws of ancient Rome.

An interest in the past and an interest in the present are not mutually exclusive; indeed you cannot understand either, without some understanding of both for they are not discontinuous. I wrote a play about Sir Thomas More and in America it was thought relevant to Senator McCarthy's persecution of the Left. And though Shakespeare never set a play in Elizabethan London yet Elizabethan London breathes in Shakespeare's plays. He clearly relished the life of his own time and had a decent concern for contemporary issues. But he was a man of the Theatre heart and soul, and dealt with contemporary issues at the proper theatrical distance.

Despite which, and to conclude, I have to confess a less worthy reason for writing historical plays. I would claim, like Shakespeare, to be concerned for my own times. But I am not sure that I relish them. 'Things fall apart; the centre cannot hold.' Indeed they do; I fear it can't. And I don't like it. And have a love of old things, old buildings, books, pictures and music, which I suspect is reprehensible. Are they really, as they seem to me, more human than our own new things, or older merely? There is no going back to them in any case. And now I come to think of that, I realize I wouldn't want to. I belong then to the present. Good. I wish the present were more human though, that people were not so distressed, and things were made with more respect.

ROBERT BOLT

A NOTE TO THE DESIGNER

I have tried to assume enough for you to work upon yet not so much as to prevent your making a substantial contribution to the style of production.

You will see that the stage serves at one moment for the Court of England and at the next for the Court of Scotland. I hope the properties will be solid and pleasurable in themselves to look at, but that the lighting, not the properties, will create the changes of time and place and mood. I hope the costumes will convey the extravagances and extremes of the period, yet not distract the audience nor tie up the actors.

I have assumed: one, a flat-topped pyramid or flight of shallow steps, supporting a screen or curtain in the First Act and the throne in the Second Act; two, a table with stools; three, a 'pulpit' though this could be a mere lectern; four, a hanging or revolving cloth of State. My intention is to maintain a smoothly continuous narrative to which changes of time and place will seem incidental.

PRINCIPAL CHARACTERS IN ORDER OF
THEIR APPEARANCE

NAU: An elderly bachelor; gentle, learned, anxious, utterly upright, deeply affectionate.

MARY: Overbred, refined and passionate; sympathetic, beautiful, intelligent and brave. But sensual and subjective. Born a Queen, deferred to from the cradle, it is a tribute to her nature that she is not simply spoiled. But she mistakes her public office for a private attribute.

CECIL: A top flight Civil Servant, reasonable, courteous, ruthless.

ELIZABETH: Personable, wilful, highly-strung. But schooled to clear sight and tuned to self-discipline by a dangerous and lonely childhood. Commencing her reign as a natural perhaps just faintly neurotic young woman, her strength of character is such that she meets the unnatural demands of Queenship with increasing brilliance, in an increasing rage of undisclosed resentment.

DUDLEY: A tall, hard, virile animal; unintellectual but nobody's fool.

KNOX: A pedant and a demagogue, a nasty combination. But palpably, frighteningly sincere.

MORTON: Renaissance noble and tribal Chief; seasoned and at ease in every kind of villainy.

RIZZIO: A likeable hedonist, affectionate and sceptical; but a lightweight; precarious.

BOTHWELL: Shrewd, coarse-natured, irresponsible; but uncomplaining as unpitying, genuinely a law unto himself; a dangerous vortex to dependent natures.

BISHOP: A conscientious career clergyman, a bit selfish, a bit ignoble; but he knows that.

WALSINGHAM: A Puritan and humourless on principle, but dangerously intelligent; a selfless intriguer, a dedicated wolf.

DE QUADRA: Walsingham's opposite, suave in manner; equally dedicated, equally dangerous.

DARNLEY: A tall, athletic, good looking aristocrat; too young, too merely pleasant to withstand the heavy personal and public pressures bearing on him.

ORMISTON: A ragged Border ruffian. Middle-aged, his moral sense quite atrophied.

DAVISON: A slightly built youth of good family. Too generous by nature for the trade of politics.

PRISONER: A scholar priest worn thin by the life of a secret agent.

SCOTS LAIRDS, SERVANTS, CLERKS.

CAST OF FIRST PERFORMANCE

Vivat! Vivat Regina! was first presented at the Chichester Festival Theatre, on 20 May 1970, with the following cast:

CATHERINE DE MEDICI	Mairhi Russell
MARY, QUEEN OF SCOTS	Sarah Miles
FRANCOIS II, KING OF FRANCE	Michael Feast
THE CARDINAL OF LORRAINE	William Hutt
ELIZABETH I OF ENGLAND ·	Eileen Atkins
WILLIAM CECIL	Richard Pearson
ROBERT DUDLEY	Norman Eshley
JOHN KNOX	Leonard Maguire
BAGPIPER	Willie Cochrane
LORD MORTON	Archie Duncan
DAVID RIZZIO	Barry Jackson
LORD BOTHWELL	David McKail
CLAUD NAU	Charles Lloyd Pack
A BISHOP	Brian Hawksley
A CLERIC	Robin Humphreys
SIR FRANCIS WALSINGHAM	Edgar Wreford
DE QUADRA	Edward Atienza
A MESSENGER	Michael Feast
HENRY STUART, LORD DARNLEY	James Warwick
LORD MAR	Cyril Wheeler
A DOCTOR	Roger Rowland
TALA	Charles Houston
ORMISTON	Jonathan Mallard
DAVISON	Philip Anthony
EARL OF SHREWSBURY	Brian Hawksley
A PRISONER	Charles Houston
FRANCIS, DUKE OF ALENCON	Milo Sperber
RUTHVEN	Leon Greene
LINDSAY	Thick Wilson
FALCONSIDE	Raymond Skipp
KERR	Antony Milner
DOUGLAS	Jonathan Mallard
AN ARCHBISHOP	Kenneth McClellan
PHILIP, KING OF SPAIN	Antony Milner
THE POPE	Robert Selbie
A PRIEST	John Herrington
JAILERS	David Gwillim: Raymond Skipp
BREWER	David Gwillim
COURTIERS, LAIRDS, CLERKS, SERVANTS	David Gwillim: John Herrington: Carolyn Lyster: Melinda May: John O'Brien: Mary Savage: Raymond Skipp: Cyril Wheeler

The Play was Directed by PETER DEWS
Designed by CARL TOMS
Music Composed and Arranged by RICHARD KAYNE

The Chichester Festival Production of *Vivat! Vivat Regina!* in the revised text, was presented by H. M. Tennent Ltd. and John Clements Plays Ltd at the Piccadilly Theatre, London, on 8 October 1970, with the following cast:

MARY, QUEEN OF SCOTS	Sarah Miles
CLAUD NAU	David Bird
WILLIAM CECIL	Richard Pearson
ELIZABETH I OF ENGLAND	Eileen Atkins
ROBERT DUDLEY	Norman Eshley
JOHN KNOX	Leonard Maguire
BAGPIPER	Willie Cochrane
DAVID RIZZIO	Matthew Guinness
LORD MORTON	Archie Duncan
LORD BOTHWELL	David McKail
LORD BISHOP OF DURHAM	Brian Hawksley
A CLERIC	Kenneth Caswell
SIR FRANCIS WALSINGHAM	Edgar Wreford
DE QUADRA	Edward Atienza
DAVISON	Eilian Wyn
HENRY STUART, LORD DARNLEY	Cavan Kendall
LORD MAR	Brian Hawksley
RUTHVEN	Glyn Grain
LINDSEY	Alexander John
A DOCTOR	Ken Grant
TALA	Malcolm Rogers
ORMISTON	Jonathan Mallard
A PRISONER	Malcolm Rogers
SCOTS ARCHBISHOP	Maurice Jones
PHILIP, KING OF SPAIN	Alastair Meldrum
THE POPE	Kenneth Caswell
JAILERS	Adrian Reynolds: Ken Grant
BREWER	Adrian Reynolds
COURTIERS, LAIRDS, CLERKS, SERVANTS	Glyn Grain: Ken Grant: Maurice Jones: Alastair Meldrum: Adrian Reynolds
COURT LADIES	Isabel Metliss: Angela Easton

The Play was Directed by PETER DEWS
Designed by CARL TOMS
Lighting by MICK HUGHES
Music Composed and Arranged by RICHARD KAYNE

ACT ONE

Exterior. Dappled sunlight on leaves and fruit. NAU *stands looking up at them. Everything still. A* VOICE, *off:*

VOICE: Ho there—The Queen!

Fanfare. MARY *enters swiftly followed by two* LADIES. *She comes to a halt and looks at him. He goes down on one knee.*

NAU: Your Grace.

MARY *stares at him a space then softly, shocked and pitying:*

MARY: Oh . . .

He smiles.

NAU: Your Grace?

MARY: You are grown quite white, Claud.

He smiles again at the note of reproach, rubs his white hair, rises and, ruefully:

NAU: The winters in Scotland are frosty.

Her faint smile vanishes. She crosses away from him.

MARY: Yes . . . Upon what care of State I wonder has my mother sent you back to France. I'm sure it is some care of State. No care for me.

NAU: (*Reproving*) Mignon: before all else I am to tell you that your mother loves you well.

MARY: My mother does not know me.

NAU: That is her sorrow too. The ruling of your Scottish kingdom in your name—and nothing else—has kept your mother from you. And Mignon, that is love and not the lack of it.

MARY: A kind of love.

NAU: The hardest kind.

MARY: Aye hard it is. And granite too is hard. But I have yet to hear it is a good material to make a cradle of. I tell you, Claud, no care of State shall keep me from my child. . . (*Disturbed, she controls her feelings, sits, formal*): Come, let me know your charges.

NAU: Mignon, your mother wonders whether presently in probability you may yourself expect a child.

She looks at him. Softly:

MARY: By Heaven I wonder she should wonder it. By Christ— I wonder you should ask!

NAU: (*Appalled*)—Mignon—

MARY: —Leave us, ladies.

LADIES *curtsey, exit quickly.*

NAU: —Mignon—

MARY: —I was your 'mignon' when I was your pupil, sir!

NAU: (*Bewildered*) Your Grace, I meant no disrespect—

MARY: What did you mean—affection?

NAU: Assuredly, Your Grace.

MARY: I do not understand you, Claud.

She leaves him.

Have you not waited on my husband?

NAU: But now, Your Grace.

MARY: Did you not see his face—?—They sometimes draw the curtains, Claud, to spare his visitors his face.

NAU: I saw, Your Grace.

MARY: And having seen his face—And having seen the suppurating sores that batten on his poor young mouth—And having seen his ancient eyes—Sir, do you ask? do you of all men dare to ask if presently in probability I may expect a child?

He stares at her a second. Understands her misconception.

NAU: O-o-oh . . . (*He kneels*) Pardon.

MARY: No!

(*But seeing his pathetic kneeling figure:*)

Oh Claud, I was a little girl, and you were all the father and the mother that I had; you taught me how to read and write; and when I got my lessons well—Good God, you sat me on your

knee and said I was your best of little girls!... And when I got
my lessons ill my sharpest punishment was your displeasure!
And you stood by and said no word and let them marry me to
syphilis! No no—you shall not have my pardon now.

NAU: My word carries no weight, Your Grace. Beseech Your
Grace believe I spoke.

She looks at him dubiously, suspiciously:

MARY: You spoke no word to me.

NAU: They said it would be treason and the axe if I should speak
that word, to you. And I was too afraid to do my duty. Pardon.

After a pause, gently

MARY: Pardon? For what?

NAU: Cowardice.

She crosses; raises him.

MARY: I'm glad that it was cowardice. Connivance I could not
have pardoned.

NAU: And am I pardoned now?

MARY: Right gladly. (*She becomes almost shy*) I wept in puddles
when you went away to Scotland, Claud.

NAU: I wept a little too.

MARY: Truly?

NAU: I wept with due decorum but, oh yes, I wept.

MARY (*smiling*): 'With due decorum'. Oh welcome back ... It
was my mother offered you the axe if you should tell me, was
it not?

NAU: It was.

MARY: For love of me?

NAU: She made the match for love of you. Your husband is the
King of France. You are the Queen of Scots. And France and
Scotland joined might get your English Kingdom too.

MARY: Would you, for fifty Englands, kiss my husband on the
mouth?

He cannot meet her eyes. Looks after her as she leaves him.

NAU: Can they not cure him, Madam?

MARY: If prayer and care can cure him, I will do it. I do not think the doctors can.

NAU: God Bless Your Grace.

MARY: Aye, bless me, Claud. I also pray for him to die.

NAU: Mignon!

MARY: Yes. And for myself to have a husband I might love.

NAU: Nay now, you must love the one you have.

MARY: I am forbid to touch him, Claud.

NAU: There is a love that needs no touching.

MARY: With such a love as that I love him. But what kind of 'love' is that?

NAU: The royal kind. The King of Heaven loves us all with such a love as that.

MARY: I know it, sir. (*Crosses herself.*) And holy nuns return his love; but then they are betrothed to Christ. My husband was betrothed to death upon the day that he was born. And I have no such high vocation as a nun.

NAU (*stern*): You ought to have; you have high office.

MARY: I know that too, sir. (*Leaving him.*) Right well I know. (*She is abstracted.*) . . . What is your second charge?

NAU: Nay let us finish with the first—(*Severe.*) Mignon, do you mean to take a lover?

MARY: . . . I mean to hear your second charge.

NAU: The treaty which your mother has negotiated with the English.

Indifferent, her thoughts elsewhere—

MARY: Well?

NAU: The English have desired another term.

MARY: Oh?

NAU: Your Grace shows here (*he indicates the cloth of state*) the lion of Scotland and the English leopard.

She begins to pay attention.

MARY: Yes?

NAU: The English now desire you to take down the leopard and show the lion only.

MARY: No.

NAU: Your Grace, it is the express desire of the English Queen.

MARY: Of whom?

NAU: Your Grace, she is effectively the Queen.

MARY: Elizabeth fitz Tudor is a bastard and a heretic and cannot be a Queen.

NAU: She sits on a throne.

MARY: A dog can do that. No, I will not sign this treaty, Claud.

NAU: Then the English army will remain in Scotland, where it lives right barbarously on the common people.

MARY: You are clever, Claud.

NAU: Your Grace, I hope, is pitiful.

MARY: Let her be pitiful—It is her army!

NAU: They are your people.

MARY (*shrugs*): Well I will sign it. And she is Queen indeed.

NAU: In this you show more Queen than she.

MARY: Aye anything that makes me less makes me more Queen, Claud, does it not?

NAU: There is much truth in that.

MARY: There is no truth at all in that. And I am sick of hearing that. Diminish me, the Queen's diminished. Starve me and the Queen will fail. If I am sickly, she is pale. I am the Queen and more the Queen the *more* I am myself!

It is a credo, passionate. He looks at her thoughtfully and then:

NAU: So thinks Elizabeth.

MARY (*sour indifference*): Indeed.

NAU: Indeed. She too mistakes her office for herself. And thinks that her whole duty is to do as she desires.

MARY: She has not had the advantage of your ceaseless moralizing, Claud.

NAU: Perhaps that's it. For she will have what she desires and it will fetch her off the throne.

MARY (*startled*): What—?—Why what does she desire?

NAU: A husband she might love.

MARY: What husband?

NAU: Her lover.

MARY (*incredulous*): Robert Dudley?

NAU: She loves him.

MARY: But he's a Commoner.

NAU: She loves him for himself, perhaps.

MARY: He has a wife.

NAU: He does not love his wife.

MARY: So?

NAU (*suddenly stern, heavy with distaste*): So his wife must die.

MARY: . . . How, die?

NAU: Violently.

MARY: Are they mad?

NAU: They see no duty but their duty to themselves. And that is mad.

MARY: Oh let them do it . . . Let them do it!

NAU: Can you rejoice at murder?

MARY: Nay Claud, you said yourself this thing will fetch her off the throne.

NAU: The Queen then must rejoice. I had thought *yourself* more natural.

MARY: You are my teacher still . . . But is it true?

NAU: Your mother thinks it true.

MARY: I'll warrant she rejoices at it. (*Then seeing something in his face:*) What is it, Claud?

NAU: Your mother does not much rejoice at anything, Your Grace.

MARY: Why?

NAU: Your Grace, she is dying.

MARY: Oh.

  She moves, checks, sharply:

  You should have told me this at first.

NAU: I was instructed to retain it till the last.

MARY: Why?

NAU: Your royal mother charged me thus: She said: 'Our daughter must think first upon these high affairs of state, not discomposed by any grief she may be pleased to feel, upon our dying.'

She stares at him. Softly:

MARY: She said that?

NAU: Your Grace.

MARY (*almost whispering*): Dying, she said *that*?

NAU: Your Grace.

MARY: Oh Claud—I would to God that I had known her!

Her face crumples, streaming with silent tears she raises and lets fall her arms in a gesture of utter helplessness, and goes, blindly. He looks after her.

NAU: Oh too much passion, too much.

He collects himself, going quickly after her, calls formal:

Ho there—The Queen!

Fanfare. He exits. Light change to cold interior as leaves and flowers fly out. SERVANTS *enter, place table and throne.* CECIL *enters.*

CECIL: Ho there—the Queen!

Fanfare. ELIZABETH *makes a royal entrance.* SERVANTS *bow and exit as she sits.*

CECIL: Your Grace, even a sovereign cannot do what is impossible.

ELIZABETH: For me to marry Robert Dudley is not impossible.

CECIL: For Your Grace to marry him and remain Queen of England is impossible. (*Gentle insistence.*) He must to prison.

ELIZABETH: We do not know yet that he did it!

CECIL: It would appear that he did it. That being so it must be made apparent that Your Grace did not. Your Grace must think how such a marriage would be taken in France and Spain, as well as here at home.

ELIZABETH: Must I marry to please France and Spain?

CECIL: Your Grace, this marriage would delight them. When Mary Stuart heard of it she cried out: 'Let them do it!'

ELIZABETH: She said that?

CECIL: That and more, Your Grace.

ELIZABETH: What more?

CECIL: Such stuff as I cannot repeat to Your Grace.

ELIZABETH: She is free in her ways, that Mary.

CECIL: She can afford to be, Your Grace. She is Queen of France, and France is rich. She is Queen of Scots, and Scotland is the rear gate to England. The Catholic half of England thinks that she is Queen of England too . . . And she cried out 'Let them do it!'

ELIZABETH: Well; I would not delight Mary by my marriage. Nor will I not marry to displease her! I will marry as my heart and conscience say.

CECIL: Conscience . . . ! In Spain they are saying openly: 'What kind of a State Church is this, where the Head of the State, the Head of the Church, will not only let a man murder his wife—but marry him for't?' . . . Your Grace, he must to prison.

ELIZABETH: But what if he is innocent?

CECIL: He must to prison pending an enquiry which will find him innocent.

ELIZABETH: Call him. (CECIL *going*.) William. (*He stops*.) What if he is guilty?

CECIL: In that case too he must to prison pending an enquiry, which will find him innocent. In neither case can Your Grace marry him.

ELIZABETH: Call him.

CECIL: Be wise, Your Grace.

ELIZABETH: As wise as I can. (*And as he still hesitates, angrily:*) I cannot be wiser!

CECIL (*calls*): Robert Dudley.

DUDLEY *strides in carrying his rapier and belt. He chucks this down, glances at* CECIL, *stands bristling before* ELIZABETH, *goes down on one knee. For a moment their glances lock; then she looks away and:*

ELIZABETH: Well sir, rise, and tell it.

He rises, flashes a resentful look at CECIL *and sneers:*

DUDLEY: Haven't you been told?

ELIZABETH: Not by you.

DUDLEY: No—*I* have been kept outside your door! Three days! Three nights!

ELIZABETH: Tell it.

DUDLEY: There was a fair at Abingdon. She didn't go herself. But she sent all her servants.

CECIL: So she was alone.

DUDLEY: I didn't know she was alone; I was in London.

CECIL: Why all her servants—Was she so kind?

DUDLEY: . . . Yes.

ELIZABETH: I never heard you say so.

DUDLEY: . . . No.

CECIL: Well sir.

DUDLEY: They came back in the evening. And found her. On the floor of the hall. Below the stairs.

CECIL: With her neck broken.

DUDLEY: I was in London.

CECIL: And, your agents?

DUDLEY: What 'agents'?

CECIL: Oh come, sir.

DUDLEY: I didn't *hear* of it until that night!

CECIL: How did you hear of it?

DUDLEY: How? . . . God forgive me, right gladly.

ELIZABETH: Oh Robin.

DUDLEY: And you?

ELIZABETH: God pity me, right gladly too.

CECIL: These past six months, sir, you have put it around that your wife was sick and like to die.

DUDLEY: Yes.

CECIL: And was she?

DUDLEY: No.

CECIL: These stairs now—

DUDLEY: Elmwood. Polished.

CECIL: Ah, polished. She slipped then.

DUDLEY: I suppose so.

CECIL: It was an accident; she fell, from the stairs.

DUDLEY: I suppose so.

ELIZABETH: Robin, she was lying fifteen feet from the stairs—
She was thrown!

DUDLEY: . . . Yes! Yes. She was thrown! No, not by me. Or
by my agency. She threw herself.

ELIZABETH: Herself . . . But why?

DUDLEY: Because she *knew* that I would hear of it—right gladly.

ELIZABETH: Oh God . . .

DUDLEY: I put it around that she was sick and like to die because
I hoped—God damn me black, I hoped that one who loved me
or desired my favour might . . . do it. Well now. One who
loved me and desired my favour, *has*.

ELIZABETH: . . . Oh Robin, either this is true or else you are a
devil.

DUDLEY: You must decide that, Madam. I've done.

ELIZABETH: But can there be such love? Robin, I would not do
that for you.

DUDLEY: Well, love is never equal. I would for you.

ELIZABETH: Sir, I think this gentleman is innocent.

CECIL *is unresponsive.*

Well, speak.

CECIL: Am I to say what I think, Your Grace, or what you want
to hear?

ELIZABETH: Oh Cecil, can they never be the same?

CECIL (*shrugs*): Then I say, with Mary Stuart: 'Let them
do it'.

DUDLEY: What's this?

CECIL: Sir, the Queen believes you innocent—and I am ready
to believe you innocent—but the Queen, alas, is not the
country, nor am I—And you must understand—

DUDLEY: I understand no word you say. Can't you speak like
a man?

CECIL: To speak like a 'man', sir—If the Queen takes you to bed
she will lie down Elizabeth the First and rise the second Mrs
Dudley.

DUDLEY: . . . *Zounds!*—

He lunges for his sword.

ELIZABETH: Put that up!

She gets up, goes and stands below the cloth of state.

You may withdraw.

DUDLEY: I?

ELIZABETH: Yes, Robin.

DUDLEY: And he stays?

ELIZABETH: Yes, Robin.

He stares one moment. Snatches up his rapier, says to CECIL:

DUDLEY: Cecil, you have ruined me, and I will not
forget it.

CECIL: You are wrong, sir; I have saved you. And belike I have
made your fortune. And you will forget it.

DUDLEY *snatches a bow at* ELIZABETH, *goes.*

ELIZABETH: Cecil, were the summers better than they are now,
when you were a child?

CECIL: Your Grace—? . . . Yes, Your Grace, I share that common
illusion. The summers then were nothing but sunshine. I and
the weather have declined together.

ELIZABETH: Who raised you, Cecil?

CECIL: My father and my mother, Madam.

ELIZABETH: It is not sunshine you remember; it is love. My
father killed my mother and disowned me, and I can't
remember a summer when it was not raining after that. I
was raised by cautious strangers in the shadows, between
prisons, I was taught: Mathematics, Latin, Greek, and caution,
too well; and saw too soon where love could lead. Prisons
were familiar, and so I put my heart into protective custody.
But Cecil, I mislaid the key, and it has lain in darkness, cold
and calcifying these twenty years. And Cecil, Robin had a
magic word, which opened doors for me . . . You said that

you would be my servant and my friend, and will you be my
jailer?

    CECIL *is moved, but:*

CECIL: Something of each, Your Grace. Your Grace's Councillor.

    ELIZABETH *looks at him.*

ELIZABETH: Aye. Well then. To Council.

CECIL: And . . . the gentleman?

ELIZABETH: To prison. (*Going.*)

CECIL: Your Grace.

    She hears the discreet satisfaction in his voice and turns.

ELIZABETH: But Cecil, we believe him innocent. And if from
now until your dying day, you whisper one word to the
contrary, we will punish you.

    Light change. Thunder. Enter KNOX *in a dripping cloak; he
shakes it, water falling in a puddle at his feet. Looks up and:*

KNOX: Welcome to Scotland. And welcome to St Andrew's
Kirk, but lately called 'Cathedral'—for it isnae long since a great
fat 'bishop', in 'vestments'—like a prostitute in her under-
garments—was wont to jabber forth the Word of God in
heathen Latin from that very pulpit—Tchah!

    *He crosses to the pulpit, flips down the cross, flips up the drape, is
about to continue his address, checks, sniffs and:*

D'you know what I smell here? Scent. (*Sniffs again at the pulpit.*)
Aye, perfume. (*Looks round.*) The whole place needs scrubbin'!
It still reeks of Catholicism!

    Controls himself. Walks away.

Well well, yon fat lad'll no enjoy his 'tithes' where he is now.
We hastened him where he come from (*jabbing downwards*) wi'
a length of rope. And you'll look hard for a Catholic priest in
Scotland now. Scotsmen can stand upright! We have a godly
governance . . . ! Or did until today. Today it seems once more
we have a Queen amongst us. And that's my matter.

    Crosses briskly to pulpit and mounts.

Beloved brethren. Certain of the Ancient Fathers make a
question of it whether women have immortal souls like men
or else like animals are morsels of mere Nature.

Breaks off, leans forward, confidential:

Er, this is my First Blast of the Trumpet Against the Monstrous Regiment of Women. Yes, I John Knox that am the Father of the Kirk and spake with Calvin as a friend, regard myself as naething mair than a wee trumpet in the hands of the Almighty . . . And if that's not humility, I'd like to know what is . . .

He resumes his formal academic manner.

Now. If the Fathers make a question of it, then it is in doubt. Doubt is a lesser thing than certainty. It is a certainty that men have souls. So: Woman is a lesser thing than man.

Leans forward, impressively:

That being so, the Regiment of women *over* men is monstrous —And we must take it as a visitation and a punishment—as was proved upon us lately by that tiger Mary Guise, as proves upon the English by that wolf Elizabeth, and as will prove upon us once again by that she cat Mary Stuart, now unhappily amongst us following the death—the *mysterious* death—of her wee French husband. No more of that. They that have ears, let them hear. He was, they say, unable to supply her raging appetite.

Light change, exterior. KNOX *sits, disappearing. Enter* BAG-PIPER, *playing, followed by* MARY, *wearing crimson. She sits. She is followed by* LADIES, RIZZIO *and* NAU, *all in grey silk aflutter with white favours. Last come the* SCOTS LORDS *wearing black faintly relieved by sombre plaids. The entourage groups itself about* MARY. *The* SCOTS LORDS *stand in a stiff line behind the solemn* BAGPIPER, *who plays on.*

MARY *and entourage have difficulty in suppressing their amusement. Seeing this,* MORTON *steps forward from among the* LORDS *and jabs* BAGPIPER *in the ribs. Startled, he stops and his instrument falls silent with a long-drawn melancholy wail.*

MARY *registers the stone-faced* LORDS.

MARY: My lords, forgive us. Our ear is not yet tuned to this wild instrument.

MORTON: Certainly, Madam, it is no lute.

RIZZIO *picks out a mocking little chord on the strings of his beribboned instrument and* MARY *sharply:*

MARY: Davie—have done . . . Where is Lord Bothwell?

BOTHWELL (*steps forward*): Madam.

MARY: Here sir.

She goes and gives him a purse.

MARY: We thank you for conducting us from France in safety, through such storms.

BOTHWELL (*looking up at her*): Were there storms, Madam—?— I didn't notice.

MARY: Ah—A Scot can turn a compliment!

BOTHWELL: Aye—given a strong stimulus.

MARY: Will you remain in Edinburgh?

BOTHWELL: I am the Lord Lieutenant of the *Border*, Madam.

She sits again, straight-backed and formal.

MARY: They tell me you steal sheep across the Border, Bothwell.

BOTHWELL: Aye, Madam, English sheep.

MARY: We would not have our cousin Elizabeth provoked.

BOTHWELL: Oh they're not her sheep. They're Harry Percy's.

MARY: Lord Bothwell, we have come here to rule.

BOTHWELL: And welcome to Your Grace's bonny face.

He goes out.

MARY: Morton, this Border raiding must be stopped.

MORTON: It can't be stopped, Your Grace. Lord Bothwell is the head of the Clan Hepburn.

MARY: So?

MORTON: The Border is Hepburn country.

MARY: All Scotland is my country, my lord.

MORTON: But Your Grace has no men.

MARY: But haven't you—my Lords in Council—men?

MORTON: Aye, Madam. *We* have.

MARY: Well, no doubt we will atune ourselves to both your music and your manners. Now, we will to supper.

MORTON: Now we must to Kirk, Madam.

MARY: 'Must' we?

NAU (*quick confidential warning*): Yes.

MARY (*swallows her anger, shrugs*): Well then, to Kirk.

She rises. Light change, church interior. RIZZIO *and* NAU *move chair.* LORDS *and* ENTOURAGE *counter-march. Fall still all looking upwards at the pulpit on which the lights come up again.*

KNOX: You may read in Revelations of a Great Whore; dressed in scarlet; sitting on a throne.

A stir among the ENTOURAGE. *They look at* MARY.

MARY: If I had known your text, good Master Knox, I would have worn a different garment.

KNOX: Nae doubt.

MARY: Now that you have seen my garment, no doubt you will change your text.

KNOX: I have nae mind to.

RIZZIO: Then you insult the Queen.

KNOX: Signor Rizzio, they tell me you're Her Grace's favourite musician. What more ye may be to Her Grace, God knows. You're not a theologian. The Great Whore in the Book of Revelations is no Queen—though Queens may be great whores—she is the Church of Rome!

MARY: Now prove that, Master Knox, or by Heaven I will have God's Trumpet scoured—for I find it something dirty.

KNOX: Prove it quotha! Secret murders and strange painted vices, whispering together in the shadows of the Vatican is thought by some sufficient proof.

Murmur of approval from the LORDS.

Screeching choirs of castratos and great bronze bells to drown the outcries of the poor is thought by some sufficient proof!

A loud murmur from the LORDS. *He is intoxicated.*

Elaborate, blasphemous, tinkling show in place of sober piety is thought by some—Aye Madam, you may laugh!

MARY: Marry I must. I have heard this vulgar stuff a hundred times before and know how to refute it.

KNOX: Do so.

MARY: Shall I?

RIZZIO: —Briefly.

MARY: Suppose the Holy Father and his priests are all imperfect as you'd have them. What of that? Because there are no perfect judges, is there no such thing as justice? Priests are men, and since our father Adam fell, imperfection has been part of every man's essential nature. But it is accidental to the Church which in its essence is, was and always will be perfect.

RIZZIO: Brava! Molto brava!

KNOX (*smiles quite kindly*): Well now, my lords, it seems we are to have a little disputation here.

NAU: —No, no—

RIZZIO: —Yes—Avanti—Trounce him!

KNOX: What—Will you back your little fighting hen against John Knox?

MARY: I am willing, Master Knox.

KNOX (*kindly*): Good.

He turns away, looks over audience, manner musing, gentle, academic.

What is the essence of your Church, Your Grace?

MARY: Its essence?

KNOX: Aye. It is not—the Mass?

MARY: It is.

KNOX: What is this Mass?

MARY: It is the sacrament whereat the priest offers to God the sacrifice of Jesus Christ.

KNOX (*quickly, as not having heard*): Who offers it?

MARY: . . . It is a sacrament.

KNOX: Who offers it?

MARY: The priest.

KNOX: The priest . . .

His voice is not quite steady on the word. Then as before:

Without the sacrifice of Jesus Christ, could any soul hope for redemption?

MARY: No.

KNOX: Can God refuse that sacrifice, when it is offered?

MARY: He will not.

KNOX: Can he—?—(*Warning.*) Remembering that the Son who is sacrificed, the Father who is offered it are both—(*breathing hard now*)—one God?

MARY: . . . I see where you would lead me.

KNOX: Daren't you follow?

MARY: You are insolent!

KNOX: A very royal argument.

MARY: No. God cannot refuse it.

KNOX: Then God is at the mercy of the priest.

> *Murmur of satisfaction from the* LORDS, *but* KNOX *ascends now to a level of frightening passion, though his voice is at first low.*

And my soul is at the mercy of the priest. For we can only traffic at the priest's permission. Christ's sacrifice is a cold spring, put here for my soul to drink at freely—which else must perish in this *desert* of a world! But now the Church has led this spring into a tank, and on this tank the priest has put a tap—the Mass—by which he turns Christ's mercy on and off and sells it by the dram!

MARY: Hold there—!

KNOX: Aye Madam, hold fast will I—for he will sell it into hands still red with the murder of a husband—

> *She leaps up from her chair.*

—Hands still hot from groping, slake the thirst of carnal fever with it, ladle it down mouths still wet from filthy exercise, sell it will he—

MARY: Come down from there! By God, come down or answer for your disobedience with your *head*!

KNOX: 'By God' *she says,* blaspheming in his very house!

MARY: This is no house of God! This is a market—where a scurrilous low peasant brings his dirty produce—!—(*Whirls on the* LORDS.) And buys treason from disloyal Lords!

NAU: Madam—!

KNOX (*tolerantly*): She is young. (*He descends.*)

MARY: Quit us!

KNOX: And passionate.

MARY: Go!

> *As he crosses, the* LORDS *following:*

Ourselves we will to our own chapel—to hear Mass!

KNOX: Madam, I am sorry for you; make a marriage.

> KNOX *and* LORDS *go, she crying after them:*

MARY: Save your sorrow for yourself, John Knox! For I may make a marriage that will give this country cause for sorrow.

> ALL *go. Light change. Fanfare modulates to Organ chord.*
> BISHOP *and* CLERIC *enter, cross to pulpit, plain-chanting:*

BISHOP: God save the Queen.

CLERIC: And all the Royal Family.

BISHOP: God save the Duke and Duchess.

CLERIC: And both their charming children.

BISHOP: God save all Barons, Earls, Viscounts and Baronets.

CLERIC: And the ladies they have married.

BISHOP: God bless the Squire.

CLERIC: And the Squire's wife.

BISHOP: And the Squire's Bailiff.

CLERIC: And the Constable.

BISHOP: And the Overseer of the Highway.

CLERIC: And the Overseer of the Poor.

> *During this, they have replaced the Catholic cross and drape, been worried by the effect, replaced them with a more discreet cross and drape and congratulated one another.* BISHOP *mounts into pulpit where now he concludes.*

BISHOP: God Bless all persons in positions of authority.

> *He smiles at his congregation and begins his address.*

Steering our course between the Scylla of Rome and the Charybdis of Geneva, we in the Church of England cultivate the quality of moderation. Not one of the heroic virtues. No, compared with courage, and conviction, moderation is a modest matter. Sometimes—as I am aware—a laughing matter.

Sobeit. The block and the bonfire are not laughing matters, and I would rather be the object of your ridicule than of your fear, will gladly spend Eternity in some quite humble mansion of my Father's House if I may get there without blood or fire . . . And that, at this point in our history is not so easy as you might suppose. No I am not ashamed to lift my voice and pray:

(Plain chant.) God Save the Queen.

DUDLEY, CECIL, CLERKS *enter. Plain chanting a descant.*

ALL: A-a-a-a-a-aamen-en.

A blown up contemporary print of Whitehall, labelled, flies in over table. DUDLEY *frontstage is adjusting a new robe and chain with fierce satisfaction.* CECIL *smiles.*

CECIL: Well, sir Councillor, I said I should make your fortune.

DUDLEY: And that I should prove ungrateful. There you were wrong.

CECIL: We shall see. A word in your ear. Do not seem too ready in the business I have broached to you.

DUDLEY: No.

A VOICE *(off)*: Ho there—the Queen!

CECIL: Let me persuade you.

DUDLEY: So.

ELIZABETH *enters with* WALSINGHAM. *She affects surprise at seeing* DUDLEY.

ELIZABETH: How, Master Cecil, what does *this* fellow here?

ALL *laugh at the Queen's little joke.*

DUDLEY *(kneels)*: He kneels, serves, loves.

ELIZABETH: Well. Come then, gentlemen.

They sit. WALSINGHAM *busy with papers.*

WALSINGHAM: The New Dean for Durham. It is between Doctor Glover and Doctor Boze.

ELIZABETH: Which?

WALSINGHAM: Glover is three parts Catholic.

ELIZABETH: Walsingham for Doctor Boze.

CECIL: I also, Madam. There are too many Catholics in the North already. Too close to the Border.

WALSINGHAM *scribbles as:*

ELIZABETH: To the Lord Bishop at Durham. Reverend Father in God. We have heeded your request to name a person. Long thought and anxious prayer alike conclude in Doctor Boze. She that hath you ever in her mind and care, your loving Sovereign, Elizabeth etcetera.

As CLERK *crosses with letter to* BISHOP *in pulpit she says to* DUDLEY.

You see how we dispatch here, Councillor.

BISHOP *glances at paper.*

BISHOP: To the Queen's Majesty at Whitehall. May it please Your Grace, this Doctor Boze inclines towards Geneva and the people hereabouts alas bend hard the other way. We fear he will prove contumaceous. May it please Your Grace to think upon the Reverend Doctor Culpepper.

CLERIC *looks modest.*

This gentleman is moderate, learned, lowly, and discreet. He loves not dispute. Besides he is known to us.

Hands letter to CLERK *who takes it back to table,* CLERIC *and* BISHOP *looking anxiously after him,* BISHOP *murmuring:*

Eternally Your Grace's grateful servant Hugh, Dunelmiensis.

ELIZABETH: Reverenced Father. The multiplying merits of your nephew are known to us. Notwithstanding, further thought and yet extended prayer confirm our former choice. But we would not be peremptory.

BISHOP: It's Boze.

He sits, light down on pulpit.

WALSINGHAM: Good.

ELIZABETH: Glover is the better man.

CECIL: But Boze the better watchdog. And Your Grace has need of watchdogs on the Scottish Border, now.

ELIZABETH (*alert*): Why? What news from Scotland?

CECIL: It comes from Madrid, Your Grace. It is quite certain that the King of Spain will marry his son to Mary Stuart.

ELIZABETH: . . . Well then, it is certain.

CECIL: Your Grace, it must not be.

ELIZABETH: What then? (*He does not answer.*)

WALSINGHAM: It cannot be, Your Grace; war rather.

CECIL: War with Spain . . .?

ELIZABETH: What then? Speak!

CECIL (*hesitates then*): Spain would not marry Scotland, if he could marry here.

ELIZABETH: Cecil, I have told you not to speak of this again.

CECIL: I spoke at your command, Your Grace.

ELIZABETH: Oh Cecil, you are too clever to be honest . . .

She rises, uneasy. CECIL *presses his advantage.*

CECIL: If a Spanish army comes at us from Scotland it comes through the Catholic North. On a Catholic Crusade, with a Catholic Queen at its head. And the North won't fight . . .

ELIZABETH: And would the South accept a Catholic King? Walsingham, would you?

All look at WALSINGHAM, *and* CECIL *quickly:*

CECIL: No King; a Consort.

WALSINGHAM: He would not be offered the Crown Matrimonial?

CECIL: No.

WALSINGHAM: And a Protestant marriage?

CECIL: Of course.

WALSINGHAM: It is a way, Your Grace. If he will take those terms.

ELIZABETH: He will not.

CECIL: Then give him war, Your Grace, and then give even me a sword—but only then. An he would come by sea, we might resist. But if he comes by land what army can we send against those Spanish Infantry? We are Sunday bowmen; and they are men of iron; and they have proved themselves of such a sort that where they set their foot no grass grows, thereafter. War with Spain is England lost.

It makes a silence.

ELIZABETH: And the Prince of Spain is a dribbling dwarf! A diminutive monster who foams at the mouth!

CECIL: I cannot answer for his person, Majesty; I will answer for my policy.

DUDLEY *shifts.*

ELIZABETH: Aye, what do you think, Councillor Robin?

DUDLEY: Too much to speak, Your Grace.

ELIZABETH: Then quit my Council.

DUDLEY: Robin thinks, war rather, death rather, let England go. Your Grace's Councillor thinks no, let love go; Her Grace must keep England.

ELIZABETH *shifts, looks away; harshly:*

ELIZABETH: Love? Who spoke of love? . . . (*Holds out hand to* CECIL.) For Madrid. (*Glances at the paper which* CECIL *hands her.*) Who wrote this?

CECIL: I, Your Grace.

ELIZABETH: We did not think you had such wooing terms.

CECIL: I was young once, Your Grace.

ELIZABETH: Logic compels us to believe you. For Madrid—

MESSENGER *exits with letter.* DUDLEY'S *head sunk in apparent gloom.*

Cecil, what can I do for this gentleman?

CECIL: There was an Earl of Leicester once in England.

ELIZABETH: Earl—? You are very sudden friends.

CECIL: I hope it truly, Madam.

DUDLEY: Your Grace, I am not worthy.

ELIZABETH: Then be so, Lord Earl. (*Raises her voice.*) We will receive the King of Spain's reply at Hampton.

CECIL *and* DUDLEY *rise and bow. Whitehall flies out as Hampton Court flies in.* CECIL *and* DUDLEY *meanwhile meet frontstage, while* ELIZABETH *and* WALSINGHAM *'freeze'.*

CECIL: Well, sir, I had not thought you were so politic.

DUDLEY: Neither had I. I do not relish this.

CECIL: We dig for gold because we relish gold, sir. Not because we relish digging. Do you want to break off?

DUDLEY: No.

CECIL: Come then. (*Leaving.*)

DUDLEY: What is my part this time?

CECIL: Perfect silence. Come.

They approach the table, bow together and together:

CECIL: ⎱ Your Grace. (*And sit.*)
DUDLEY: ⎰

ELIZABETH: You arrive together, gentlemen.

CECIL: We met on the road, Your Grace. Is the Spanish Ambassador come?

ELIZABETH (*to* CLERK): Admit him.

Enter DE QUADRA. *Crosses swiftly, kisses her hand with affectionate respect.*

ELIZABETH: De Quadra. How does your master?

DE QUADRA: Your Grace. His Catholic Majesty is all transported. He thinks Madrid a little town in Paradise. And only fears to have curtailed his future lot by tasting Heaven here.

ELIZABETH: We thank His Majesty. And, His Majesty's fair son?

DE QUADRA: His son! Your Grace, a heart of thistledown. He floats.

ELIZABETH: Then we shall float together; for we are even as you say he is.

DE QUADRA: *Madam* . . .

CECIL: What dowry does His Majesty propose?

DE QUADRA: Ah Cecil, my good friend, the King would dower such a match with the whole world—

CECIL: —But failing that.

DE QUADRA whips out a roll of paper and places it deftly into CECIL'S hands, gliding on to ELIZABETH in the same movement.

DE QUADRA: This (*a locket*) is a likeness of the Prince.

ELIZABETH: His Highness is well favoured, if this speaks true.

DE QUADRA: Would it might, Your Grace, but alas it is not the handwork of a god.

ELIZABETH: De Quadra, such a face presages a strong mind.

DE QUADRA: Even so.

ELIZABETH: Deal honestly, De Quadra.

DE QUADRA: Your Grace, His Highness it is true is—highly-strung—But there, what would you ? The spirit of a giant in a little human frame.

ELIZABETH: How little?

DE QUADRA: His Highness is compact, Your Grace. I would not say *little* . . .

ELIZABETH: Would you say tall?

DE QUADRA: Tall . . . Alas, Your Grace, how tall is tall ?

ELIZABETH: This gentleman is tall.

> DUDLEY *rises.* CECIL *looks up from the scroll.*

CECIL: This is well.

DE QUADRA: I think so too, sir.

CECIL: Yet not so well that it could not be better. What is this of Spanish galleys in our Channel ports?

WALSINGHAM: What? That sounds more like war than wedding !

DE QUADRA: Ah, Master Walsingham, how do you do? (*To* ELIZABETH.) The galleys are for use against His Majesty's rebellious subjects in the Netherlands.

WALSINGHAM: Our best trade is with the Netherlands, Your Grace.

DE QUADRA: It will be better, when the Netherlands are pacified.

WALSINGHAM: The Netherlanders are good friends to England, and to God.

DE QUADRA: With deference, Master Walsingham, they may be your friends; God selects his own. And as for England—are rebel subjects anywhere good friends to any sovereign?

ELIZABETH: Spanish galleys in our ports might make me rebel subjects here, Your Excellency.

DE QUADRA: Well well. The galleys are a lesser matter.

ELIZABETH: You have a greater?

DE QUADRA: The form of marriage.

CECIL: English.

DE QUADRA: With a Catholic marriage first.

> *It is half a question, half an assertion.*

CECIL: After.

DE QUADRA: Then immediately after.

WALSINGHAM: Why immediately?

DE QUADRA (*shrug*): The same day.

WALSINGHAM: Why the same day?

DE QUADRA (*testy*): Before the *night*, good Master Walsingham
    ... In Catholic eyes your English form of marriage would be—
    (*Spreads his hands, delicately*)—a form.

WALSINGHAM: As would the Catholic form in English eyes.

DE QUADRA: *Some* English eyes.

He says it significantly and looks at CECIL.

CECIL: Immediately after.

DE QUADRA: Excellent. The—er—form of the form is important
    too. Your Grace must know—for I alas am told to tell Your
    Grace—my master will not have his son's soul jeopardized by
    any form which makes a mock of God.

ELIZABETH: Then tell your master that we think ourselves as
    careful of our soul as any king in Christendom and would
    permit no form which mocked at God!

DE QUADRA: Your English Church is, er, flexible, Your Grace.
    Here is one thing, there another. Here a priest who is almost a
    Catholic, there a priest who is no-one knows what. There have
    lately been some church appointments, as that of Doctor Boze
    at Durham, which have much dismayed my master.

ELIZABETH: Zounds sir, will you make our church appointments
    now?

DE QUADRA: Oh dear. Of course these vexious questions would
    not be, if His Highness were to wed some Catholic Queen.

He lets it hang. CECIL *and* DUDLEY *look at* ELIZABETH.
She sighs, raises voice and:

ELIZABETH: To the Lord Bishop at Durham!

Lights up on pulpit. BISHOP *attentive.*

Reverend Father in God. We have reconsidered your wise
words concerning Doctor Boze. The man is disputatious. If

therefore it is not too late, appoint instead the Reverend
Doctor Glover—

BISHOP: Glover—!—Your Grace, the man's a rampant Papist!

ELIZABETH: —You see from this that weighed against her care
for you and for the spiritual welfare of her realm, no sacrifice
of vain consistency is too much for your loving Sovereign,
Elizabeth, etcetera.

BISHOP: The woman's mad!

Lights out on pulpit as he sits.

DE QUADRA: Excellent. And who can say but that the tender
influence of love will heal up these unhappy differences, his
golden dart transfixing two young hearts make one of two
great kingdoms. The galleys are a matter for negotiation,
naturally.

CECIL: Naturally.

DE QUADRA: May I enjoy your company tonight?

CECIL: Tonight I am engaged, Your Excellency.

DE QUADRA: Tomorrow then?

CECIL: Tomorrow I shall be in Canterbury.

DE QUADRA: Well let us not delay too long. Youth will be
served. Your Grace, I go now to write that which will transport
my master; would I had words worthy of my theme. (*He
makes a graceful bow and to* CECIL, *backing:*) Next week perhaps?

CECIL: Your Excellency's servant.

DE QUADRA: Madam, you have made me happy. (*Another bow.*)

ELIZABETH: Then we are quits.

DE QUADRA: Madam. (*Another bow; he is almost gone.*)

ELIZABETH: Your Excellency. (*He stops.*) We had thought your
Prince had lost his heart to the Queen of Scots.

DE QUADRA: The—? Your Grace, the Queen of Scots? Who
remembers the pale moon, when the great sun rises?

A final bow, and he is gone.

ELIZABETH: Well, Cecil, will it do?

CECIL: I do not know, Your Grace.

WALSINGHAM: Nor I, Your Grace. I think they mean to make us clients.

ELIZABETH: I think it will not do. And thank God for it.

CECIL: Madam, it must seem to do; until the Queen of Scots has married elsewhere.

ELIZABETH: Then let her marry soon.

CECIL: I think she will.

ELIZABETH: Perhaps we can arrange a marriage for her.

CECIL: That would be best, Your Grace. I have intelligence from Scotland coming to Nonsuch.

ELIZABETH: Mp. To Nonsuch then.

Hampton out. Nonsuch in. DUDLEY *and* CECIL *front stage.* ELIZABETH *and* WALSINGHAM *'freeze'.*

CECIL: Well, my lord, the dice are falling in our favour. Are you ready for your final throw?

DUDLEY: Cecil, why are you doing this?

CECIL: Because it is good policy for England.

DUDLEY: And what is it for Cecil?

CECIL: Good policy too. You have her heart and always will.

DUDLEY *grips him hard by the arm and growls desperately.*

DUDLEY: Then why may I not marry *here*?

CECIL: That, over my grave; the other I will help you to. Will you have it?

DUDLEY (*drops his hand*): Yes.

CECIL: To it then. You that way, I this.

They approach the table from different directions and meet there.

DUDLEY (*sitting*): Well met, Master Cecil.

CECIL: My lord. (*Sitting.*)

ELIZABETH: How is de Quadra?

CECIL: He languishes a little, but we keep him in good heart. We feed him promises.

ELIZABETH: 'We'?

CECIL: My lord had dinner with de Quadra and myself the other day.

ELIZABETH: You are grown quite intimate.

CECIL (*with a little laugh and half bow to* DUDLEY): Oh, I—would not say 'intimate'.

ELIZABETH: You sound like de Quadra. Admit the messenger from Scotland.

Enter DAVISON. *He kneels. She regards him approvingly, motions him to rise.*

So sir, the Spanish embassy to Scotland is gone home.

DAVISON: Yes, Your Grace.

ELIZABETH: And how likes that the Queen of Scots?

DAVISON: She is enraged, Your Grace.

ELIZABETH (*a grunt of satisfaction*): Ha. And does her rage become her?

DAVISON: Yes, Your Grace. All moods become her.

He says it defiantly. She stares and:

ELIZABETH: God's death, send no more *young* ambassadors to Scotland, Cecil.

She gets up, goes and examines DAVISON *as an object of deep, half-amused interest.*

ELIZABETH: Describe her then.

DAVISON: Your Grace, I cannot.

ELIZABETH: Cannot? Is she tall?

DAVISON: As Your Grace.

ELIZABETH: Thin?

DAVISON: As Your Grace.

ELIZABETH: We are twins?

DAVISON: No, Your Grace.

ELIZABETH: What colour is her hair?

DAVISON: Your Grace, her hair is shadow coloured.

ELIZABETH: God's death, he's written poetry! Her eyes?

DAVISON: Her eyes change colour with her moods, Your Grace.

ELIZABETH: You seem much taken with her moods. Has she many?

DAVISON: Yes, Your Grace.

ELIZABETH: Aye, sometimes she is right childish, is she not?

DAVISON: Yes, Your Grace. And sometimes—(*Breaks off.*)

ELIZABETH: Well?

DAVISON: Right royal, Your Grace.

ELIZABETH: Hoo! And sometimes, as we hear, she is sportive, hey? Gallante, hey? Wanton?

DAVISON: Yes, Your Grace. And cruel and wilful and unfair. But then there come such sudden sinkings, such declension into soft submission, as sets a man on a high horse.

His voice vibrates with an emotion too serious to laugh away. She leaves him, on a shaky laugh.

ELIZABETH: God's death, it ought not to be hard to find a suitor for the lady, Cecil.

She turns to find CECIL *and* DUDLEY *making furious faces at* DAVISON. CECIL *with fists raised above his head. He converts the motion hastily into a stroking of his hair as she turns, but she:*

ELIZABETH: What? What's this?

Looks at DAVISON.

What? (*Snort of mirth.*) You think we are jealous of this moon calf?

She seats herself. More formally:

What is this mountebank, Rizzio?

DAVISON: Her playfellow, Your Grace.

ELIZABETH: No more?

DAVISON: Her Councillor, Your Grace.

ELIZABETH: No more?

DAVISON: I do not know, Your Grace. But I do not think he is the man that she would love.

ELIZABETH: Why not? Come, we are not angry with you. (*She smiles.*) Why is Signor Rizzio not the man that she would love? Is he ugly?

DAVISON: It is not that, Your Grace. (*He looks at her and ventures a half-smile in response to hers.*) He is small.

ELIZABETH: Ah . . . like you.

She goes to him and rubs his hair.

The Queen of Scots likes tall men, does she?

DAVISON: Yes, Your Grace.

ELIZABETH: Poor boy. (*Then briskly, cheerfully:*) Well then
Master Cecil, it seems that we are looking for a tall—

*Breaks off and freezes. The life drains from her motionless body.
She looks at* CECIL, *at* DUDLEY, *back to* CECIL. *He bows his
head. She comprehends it all. She looks away. White-faced she
breathes out:*

O-o-o-oh . . .

She looks quickly at DUDLEY *with a last flash of hope. But now
he too bows his head and again:*

O-o-o-oh . . .

Her empty eyes wander to DAVISON.

You sir, get you gone; you are love-sick.

He goes.

Oh, Cecil.

CECIL: Your Grace—

ELIZABETH: I *see* it, Cecil, I *see* it's very good. Protestant,
English, loyal, a nobleman to boot—Earl of Leicester. And,
tall . . . It should do well . . . Eh . . .? Robin?

DUDLEY: Your Grace, I am green in Council—these gentlemen
are better able—

ELIZABETH: —*Faugh*—!

She gestures.

Go.

DUDLEY *going.*

Go both.

CECIL *follows. They escape like schoolboys. She gently
contemplates.*

Oh Robin . . .

WALSINGHAM *discreetly gathering papers, going.*

You are going, sir?

WALSINGHAM: I thought Your Grace might wish to stay this
business until . . . (*His voice tails.*)

ELIZABETH: Do you presume to know what we might
wish?

He sits, very quietly.

What business?

WALSINGHAM: A conspiracy against Your Grace's life, of Catholic gentlemen, in the County of Durham.

ELIZABETH: Against my life?

WALSINGHAM: Yes, Your Grace.

ELIZABETH: Well. Tell Cecil.

WALSINGHAM: Your Grace. (*Going.*)

ELIZABETH: In the county of Durham?

WALSINGHAM: Yes, Your Grace.

She nods. He goes. She looks at DUDLEY'S *empty chair.*

ELIZABETH: Oh . . . Councillor . . .

She raises her head and softly begins. Softly lights come up on pulpit and the gravely listening BISHOP *there.*

To the Lord Bishop at Durham. Good Father, we trouble you much. But both the gentlemen that we have named are too extreme, for this time, and that place. Therefore, let it be your kinsman's. For you tell us that he is a man of balance. And we are like a sleepwalker who wakes to find herself on a high roof, in darkness . . . and without a hand to hold her. Forgive, Elizabeth, etcetera . . .

She is going out on the last words, her hand just momentarily placed on DUDLEY'S *chair before passing on as* BISHOP *hurries down from pulpit, subdued but urgent:*

BISHOP: May it please Your Grace, my nephew is gone from here and is presently in Bristol where—

ELIZABETH (*ringingly*): Lord Bishop!

She whirls.

Do as we command or by God we will unfrock you!

She takes a great gasp of air and almost shouts:

Elizabeth! *Queen!*

Fanfare; she exits. Nonsuch flies out. Fanfare. Light change; MARY *enters. She is on* CECIL'S *arm.* NAU, LADIES, *and* RIZZIO *follow. She seats herself.*

MARY: Cecil, you are very welcome. We hear you are the wisest

Councillor in Christendom. We think our cousin kind to part
with you. The more so as we know her pleasant purpose.

CECIL: Your Grace, her purpose is most pleasant, yes.

MARY: Aye, for you are sent we hear to crack a joke with us.
But we must warn you, sir, the edge is off it, for it is foretold.

CECIL: A joke, Your Grace?

MARY: Oh. Davie, we are misinformed. Forgive me, sir. There
was a waggish fellow here the other day who said your
purpose was to offer me the hand of Robert Dudley.

CECIL: Madam, that is my purpose.

MARY: How straight he keeps his face! Excellent, sir. If you were
not a Councillor you could be a comedian.

CECIL: Indeed, Your Grace, I so lack comedy I cannot understand
how you can find the offer comic.

MARY: Sir, do not persist. Your offer is an insult—

CECIL: Your Grace?

MARY: Cecil, was Robert Dudley unfit for Elizabeth? And yet
is fit for me?

CECIL: Nay now I am quite confounded. Unfit for my mistress?
She never thought of him, Your Grace. He has her high regard
indeed but, no no, not her heart.

MARY: No, that she has given to the Prince of Spain.

CECIL: That is correct, Your Grace.

MARY: We wish him joy of such a heart. We wish her joy of
such a husband. And for her comfort tell your mistress that
we have given our heart to an Englishman.

CECIL: . . . May I know his name?

MARY: His name is Darnley.

CECIL: Now it is Your Grace who jests, I hope, for if this is not
jest it is high treason.

MARY: Sir, I am a sovereign and can commit no treason unless
against myself.

CECIL: You will find that you have done that, Madam, if you
wed Lord Darnley. I have seen the man, Your Grace has not
—he is a ladyfaced horseman, empty and idle.

MARY: Oh—It is on our account that you oppose it? We thank you for your care.

CECIL: My opposition matters nothing, Madam, but my mistress has forbidden it; for reasons you know well.

MARY: I do not study Elizabeth's reasons. But can guess them. Lord Darnley is a Catholic.

CECIL: Yes, Madam.

MARY: And bears the Tudor blood.

CECIL: Yes, Madam.

MARY: Aye—and better Tudor blood than hers because it is legitimate.

CECIL: Madam, you forget yourself.

MARY: I forget nothing. England remembers more than you suppose, and Europe knows that any child of mine by Darnley would be heir to the English throne. These are Elizabeth's reasons. And mine.

CECIL: Well, Madam, I am sorry for it, And I counsel you to put it from your mind. Lord Darnley is forbidden to quit England and will not come if you call him.

MARY: Call him.

NAU: Lord Darnley.

DARNLEY *enters.* CECIL *aghast. Then softly:*

CECIL: You fool . . .

MARY: Quit Scotland, sir, you are an uncouth messenger.

CECIL *bows curtly, going, stopped by:*

And tell your mistress that I have one reason more than she. (*Takes* DARNLEY'S *hand.*) I love this bonny gentleman.

CECIL: I think you are deceived, Your Grace. I think that you are angry with my mistress. That bonny gentleman is light. And I think that when you are undeceived you will find his passing heavy.

MARY: God's death, sir, have you finished?

CECIL: That is for Your Grace to say.

MARY: You have finished.

CECIL *goes, escorted by* NAU *and* RIZZIO.

MARY: Well, if that was Cecil, Elizabeth is welcome to him. Good Lord! I think she must have run him up from odds and ends left over from a funeral.

DARNLEY: I thought he spoke well.

MARY: He is a politician, Harry; speaking well's his trade. You were not moved by what he said?

DARNLEY: Weren't you?

MARY: I have forgotten what he said.

DARNLEY: He called me fool and said I was not fit for you.

MARY: The more fool he.

DARNLEY: Nay, all the world accounts him wise—and me unfit for you.

MARY: My love, I have not found you so—

DARNLEY: You have not wished to find me so.

MARY: You are too thoughtful, sir.

DARNLEY: I never was accounted that.

MARY: Then what has made you so? Is it my rank?

DARNLEY: My breeding fits me for your rank. Yourself has made me thoughtful.

MARY: Oh. If thought is all I have roused in you, I have wasted many pains.

DARNLEY: Nay, you have roused my love.

MARY: Be careless then, not thoughtful. You know that I love you.

DARNLEY: I know you would.

MARY: Harry, I have told you, and I swear before the Saints: I'll have a husband I can love, or else I will have none at all.

DARNLEY: Would you have loved the Prince of Spain?

MARY: Nay do not shame me, love. That was to have been a stroke of State. Yet Harry, even him I would have tried to love.

DARNLEY: And now you are trying to love me.

MARY: My lord, we were so born that we must choose fit marriage mates politically. It is God's generosity that we have found fit mates we naturally love. We are not to scrutinize

his generosity, we are to love. If we attend to love, my lord,
both dignity and reputation will come begging at our door.

Uplifted he goes to her. They kiss.

Oh come, my love—and let's be married!

*Bells, cheering and cheerful organ on speaker. She takes him by
the hand and leads him towards the upper level.* RIZZIO, NAU,
LADIES *enter one side,* LORDS *the other.* MARY *and* DARNLEY
*kneel, facing. Rise and kiss. Court applauding, crescendo on speaker.
But the* LORDS *deliberately straddle their legs and fold their arms,
glowering.*

MARY: My lords. Will you not rejoice?

MORTON: We have no cause here to rejoice.

MARY: Are even weddings not rejoiced at then, in Scotland?

MORTON: Your Grace is wedded to a Catholic boy.

DARNLEY: Call me 'boy' and you shall have cause for regret,
Lord Morton.

   MORTON *laughs.*

What sir, do you laugh?

MORTON: Yes, I laugh.

DARNLEY: I never endured insult when I was a private man, Lord
Morton; do you think I will endure it now?

MORTON: Why, what are you now?

DARNLEY: By God sir, am I not your Lord?

MORTON: You are this lady's laddie; and no more.

DARNLEY: —Zounds—!

   He steps forward; MARY *stops him.*

MARY: —Harry—!—No—!

DARNLEY: What, am I to rule Scotland and must eat such stuff
as this?

   A little silence, then MARY, *awkwardly:*

MARY: You are to rule me, my lord, not Scotland.

   DARNLEY *glares at her. Bows stiffly. Turns his back and goes.
She half starts after him.*

Harry—!

   MORTON *laughs again. She whirls.*

Lord Morton. My Consort and myself mean you no harm. And we will give ourselves one season in which to show we mean no harm. Thereafter, we expect to see you smile . . . Harry!

She hurries after DARNLEY, *court following pell-mell.*

MORTON: Ten English pounds to ten Scots pennies, they're at one another's throats within six months.

RUTHVEN: No bet.

LORDS *go, laughing. Light change.* ELIZABETH *enters at speed,* CECIL *after. She checks. He, diffident and soothing.*

CECIL (*placating*): Your Grace of course may marry whom you will.

ELIZABETH: Oh—!—You are full of news this morning, sir.

CECIL: Within what's reasonable—And this petition, which your loving Commons most respectfully present—

ELIZABETH: —Is no petition, but an admonition! I am admonished, by the Commons, to marry—now. Not when I would, nay nor to whom I would, but to one of these that they have named, and get a child by him—and now!

CECIL: The Princes they have named they have enquired into most—

ELIZABETH: Enquired, sir—? Are they kennelmen and I their breeding bitch?

CECIL: You are their mistress, Madam, and this country's Queen.

ELIZABETH: In this I am no more than any other woman, Cecil. And I tell you that I have nor mind, nor heart, to marry now.

CECIL: Your Grace it would be very prudent, now. The Queen of Scots expects a child.

ELIZABETH (*alert*): How do you know?

CECIL: I have it from Lord Morton, Madam.

ELIZABETH: He has written?

CECIL: He is here, Your Grace.

ELIZABETH: Fetch him.

He gestures quietly into wings. MORTON *enters.*
Is this true?

MORTON: Yes, Your Grace.

ELIZABETH: She has not announced it.

MORTON: No doubt she expects to make some use of the announcement.

CECIL: She'd be a fool if she did not expect to make some use of it—It is a useful thing.

ELIZABETH: If it is so.

MORTON: I have it from a friend who is a friend of a close lady-friend of Signor Rizzio.

    ELIZABETH *picks up the petition, thoughtful.*

ELIZABETH: Is he still close friends with your Queen?

MORTON: He's been no more than that since she was married. But he is still that. It's true enough, Your Grace.

ELIZABETH: I thought that Mary and her husband were no longer bedfellows.

MORTON: They're not, not since he took to whores. But they were busy bedfellows at first.

    CECIL *looks at* ELIZABETH *expecting her to follow the main issue. But she is looking down and now looking up:*

ELIZABETH: It's true, is it, that he has taken up with whores?

MORTON: Oh aye, and common brothel whores at that.

ELIZABETH: Why?

MORTON: He's a King in a brothel. In Council he's a clown. She boxed his ears and sent him packing from the Council in the end.

ELIZABETH: She boxed his ears?

MORTON: She all but pitched him off his seat.

ELIZABETH (*shrugs*): No wonder then he took to whores.

MORTON: Her wits go out the window when she's in a rage. And she was in a hellish rage. He showed so cocky and so daft you see, so brainless—overbearing, and so greedy for his own. And she, then, was in love with him.

ELIZABETH: She never was in love with him.

MORTON: Oh yes she was, Your Grace.

ELIZABETH: She was infatuated.

MORTON: Your Grace may call it what you like. I saw it. She hung upon him like a pedlar's bag. And sometimes when they danced, she had a look upon her face, that showed as much of her as if she had been naked . . . (*He is lost for a moment.*) No woman ever looked at me like that . . .

CECIL *coughs.* MORTON *comes to.*

MORTON: She's three months gone.

CECIL: And she is nightly on her knees, Your Grace, and praying for a son. And praying for her son to be a wise and potent Prince. Of Scotland and of England too. As he is like to be, and soon, Your Grace, unless Your Gr—

ELIZABETH: Enough, enough, I am not blind.

She looks at the petition.

This is not ill-considered neither. But here they name three Catholic Princes and three Protestant. (*Puts down the petition.*) And if I go a courting any one of these, I lose the love of one half of my people.

CECIL: Your Grace may find that one half of your Court is paying court in Edinburgh presently!

She looks at him.

ELIZABETH: Do you pay court in Edinburgh?

CECIL: No Madam, I do not.

ELIZABETH: The time may come. Meanwhile tell the Commons that we will not marry, yet, but that we thank them for their care. And will remit some portion of the taxes due to us this coming year. I go a-courting with my people, Cecil.

She is going. He, irritated and anxious:

CECIL: And the son that she is praying for?

ELIZABETH: Why, on your knees, good William, and pray for it to be a girl. Three Queens on the run should finish any country.

She goes, leaving CECIL *perplexed.*

MORTON: That lassie has a long head on her shoulders.

CECIL (*preoccupied*): Yes . . . The problem is to keep it there.

MORTON: Well that may be a problem for us all, quite soon.

CECIL: It will. (*He looks at* MORTON, *who says nothing.*) So what do you intend to do, Lord Morton?

MORTON (*wolfish grin*): Me, Master Cecil? D'you really want to know?

CECIL: Perhaps not. Good-day to you, Lord Morton. (*Going.*)

MORTON: Good day to you.

> CECIL *goes.*

You creepy wee creature.

> *He turns, joins Scots* LORDS *who enter.* LADIES, RIZZIO, NAU *enter opposite. Then Fanfare.* MARY *enters, all bowing, mounts to upper level, addresses* LORDS, *smiling graciously.*

MARY: My lords, we have assembled you to hear a happy thing. You were right melancholy wedding guests but now I think you will rejoice. My lords, we are with child.

MORTON: And why should we rejoice at that?

MARY: Because you are loyal Scots.

MORTON: Aye we are Scots. And we should have a Scottish King.

MARY: If God grants me a son, you'll have a Scottish King.

MORTON: His mother for a start is French.

MARY: Sacre bleu . . .

> *She turns away impatiently but then turns back.*

My father bore the blood of Bruce. And I was born at Lithgow Castle. When I was five years old I do confess I went away to France and got my breeding there—Forgive me, it was an error of my youth. If it's offensive that my manner is still Frenchified, sobeit and good-night, I can no more. It is not for myself I ask your loyalty. My child, on whose behalf I do demand your loyalty, will be both born and bred in Edinburgh —And fully Scots as you.

MORTON: And will he so?

MARY: By parentage it's true he'll be a little French on one side, a little English on the other—

MORTON: And will he so? By parentage?

MARY: I do not think I understand you, sir.

MORTON: I think you do. Where is Lord Darnley?

MARY: I do not know, sir, where he is.

MORTON: It's odd that he's not here.

MARY: It's very odd; I did desire him to be here.

MORTON: What means his being elsewhere then?

MARY: I cannot guess his meanings, but by Heaven I will come at yours.

MORTON: My meaning is the same as his. And you can come at it in any pub in Edinburgh. This child, my lords, will be a little French on one side, aye, but on the other—(*glares at* RIZZIO)—half Italian!

> MARY *raises a hand as though to strike him, controls herself, turns away.*

RIZZIO: My lords—I swear by all the Saints—!—

MARY: What—? Will you protest it? Lord Morton, leave us. You pollute the air.

> MORTON *and* LORDS *bow, go. She turns.*

Well Claud, I have tried the patient way—

RIZZIO: —Maria.

> *He points warningly. She turns to find that* BOTHWELL *has lingered and stands now looking at her. She is a bit startled.*

MARY: Lord Bothwell.

BOTHWELL (*bows gravely*): Your Grace.

MARY: What do you want?

BOTHWELL: A private audience.

MARY: Private? Why so?

BOTHWELL: Don't be frightened.

MARY: Frightened, sir? What should I fear? Leave us, gentlemen.

NAU (*anxious*): Your Grace, it is not—

MARY: Nay leave us, Claud.

RIZZIO (*dubious*): Maria—

MARY: Va t'en.

> NAU, RIZZIO, LADIES, *go.* BOTHWELL *and* MARY *cross, slowly, eyeing one another.*

Well?

BOTHWELL: Puir wee lass.

MARY (*amused and startled*): What?

BOTHWELL: You're going to have a hard confinement. You're too thin for it, though.

MARY: Indeed?

BOTHWELL: I know what I'm talking about, too. You just bide quiet awhile. Don't ride so much; and don't ride so wild. And mind what you're eatin'. And altogether be a bit more sensible; and treat yourself more kind.

MARY: Well thanks; I will.

BOTHWELL: Guid. When's it due?

MARY: The time of our confinement is a thing we will announce when we are minded to, Lord Bothwell.

BOTHWELL: July.

MARY: Who told you that?

BOTHWELL: It wasn't very hard to guess—Your husband has been spending himself elsewhere since November, has he not?

MARY: If you will speak of him, sir, you will study your respect.

BOTHWELL: Let's speak of something else then. You'd have to study hard to speak of Darnley with respect.

MARY: I think this insolence is studied. Leave us.

BOTHWELL: Look, I have matter which you ought to hear.

MARY: I will not hear it.

He shrugs and is about to go.

Unless you can attain a minimum of manner too.

BOTHWELL: Sacre bleu! (*Mimics her.*) If my manner is offensive sobeit and good-night.

MARY: Oh Jesus, are we there again?

BOTHWELL: I like your manner fine.

She looks at him.

It's very pretty.

MARY: Good heavens, my Lord, that is the second compliment within these same four years.

BOTHWELL: Now fancy you rememberin' the first.

MARY: Remember it—? How not? A compliment in Scotland

is a memorable thing. It stands out like a lily on a heap of dung.

BOTHWELL: That's no' a bad description of yourself in Scotland.

They exchange a little mocking bow.

MARY: I'll hear your matter.

BOTHWELL: It's men and means you want, I think?

MARY: It is.

BOTHWELL: You do not mean to meddle with the Kirk?

MARY: The Kirk, sir? Are you pious?

BOTHWELL: When the Kirk threw down the Catholic Church I got some fine broad meadow land; that used to belong to the Catholic Church. I'm awfu' pious about those meadows.

MARY: If I got men and means from you, I could not meddle with your meadows.

BOTHWELL: That's true enough. What terms are you offerin'?

MARY: No terms. I have taken out an option on the future, Bothwell; and you have wit enough to see it.

BOTHWELL (*smiling approval*): You're no fool, are you?

MARY: No sir; did you think I was?

BOTHWELL: You married Darnley.

MARY: . . . What is it in me, Bothwell, that provokes you and your fellow lords at every turn and all the time to strip me of my dignity? Is it merely that I am a woman?

BOTHWELL: A bonny woman.

MARY: So?

BOTHWELL: Worth strippin'.

MARY: Is that another compliment?

BOTHWELL: Yes.

MARY: Your vein of courtesy's exhausted. Go.

    BOTHWELL *going.*

It was a compliment, sir, for a courtesan.

BOTHWELL: Am I to go or stay?

MARY: You'll change your ways, sir, if you stay.

BOTHWELL: I have no mind to change my ways. We're very much alike.

MARY: You will not tell me that's a compliment.

BOTHWELL: Oh I steal sheep and you steal revenues. Otherwise we're much alike.

MARY: By God there is another difference—

BOTHWELL: —There is—

MARY: —I am a sovereign. And you, sir, are a subject.

BOTHWELL: No. You are a woman. (*Approaches close.*) Why don't you send me packin' now?

MARY: Oh sir, I am fascinated by your rough provincial masculinity.

BOTHWELL: I think you are, a bit.

MARY: Go!

> BOTHWELL *going again.*

You are unfit for our purpose.

BOTHWELL: Why, what was that?

MARY: What sir, do you smell promotion?

BOTHWELL: Do I?

MARY: A high promotion, Bothwell; you might come by further meadows.

BOTHWELL: What then?

MARY: We had thought to make you Lord Protector to our child.

BOTHWELL: Oh. (*He pulls at his beard, thoughtfully.*)

MARY: Ay. Now I think he'll change his ways.

BOTHWELL: You'd want a Catholic for that.

MARY: So change your church and be a Catholic. It would not cost you much.

BOTHWELL: It would not cost me anything, to be a Catholic, for I am not a Christian. I will not do it, though. For if our ways are different and you would like our ways to match— you must change your ways! To mine!

MARY: By Heaven, Lord Bothwell, I have heard about your ways —Even in Scotland your name is morbid. You are a bloody villain, sir, a tyrant and a sodomist, an enemy to innocence, a vampire and a demonist! It's only in your better moments, Bothwell, that you are a thief.

BOTHWELL: So *that's* what fascinates you.

MARY: Go!

> *He goes.*

MARY: And go for ever—be banished to Dunbar—You will never see my face again!

BOTHWELL: You're wrong, I think.

MARY: *Go!*

BOTHWELL: I was goin'—you keep stoppin' me.

> *He has gone. She glares after him. Unseen behind her* NAU *and* RIZZIO *enter.*

MARY: Lout!

RIZZIO: Bothwell?

MARY: Yes. (*Turns to him with a little laugh.*) I do believe he thinks he is a lady's man!

RIZZIO: Astonishing.

MARY: No fooling, sir; I am not in the mood.

> *Light begins to concentrate into a small conspiratorial area at the table surrounded by shadow. She sits, and says to* NAU:

Did any other of the lords come forward, Claud?

NAU: No, Your Grace.

MARY (*dips pen*): Well . . . (*She writes rapidly.*) I will try my way now.

> *He sits and watches her unhappily.* RIZZIO *too draws near.*

NAU: You write, Your Grace?

MARY: Yes sir, I write.

RIZZIO (*peeping*): In Latin too.

NAU: To whom does Your Grace write?

RIZZIO: He'll have difficulty reading it, whoever he may be.

MARY (*writing*): So you will make it fair. And you (*looking up at* NAU) will carry it to Rome.

NAU (*sadly*): Oh Madam, Rome?

MARY: And when you have got means, in Rome, I will send to Milan, for mercenaries. Loyalty does not grow in Scotland, so I will import it.

> DARNLEY *enters, uncertainly, hanging off in the shadows.*

NAU: My lord.

DARNLEY (*eagerly*): Good evening, Claud . . . Signor Rizzio.

RIZZIO: My lord.

They withdraw respectfully as he drifts towards MARY, *who after one glance round, one stare, has returned to her writing. He sits and watches her.*

DARNLEY: Good evening, Mary.

MARY: What do you want?

DARNLEY: Might I not simply have come home, like any other man?

MARY: You might. It seems improbable.

She has not looked up from her flying pen. A pause:

DARNLEY: Are you writing a letter?

MARY: Yes.

DARNLEY: Who to?

She thrusts it towards him at full stretch. He looks at it.

It's in Latin.

MARY: Yes.

DARNLEY: I can't read Latin.

MARY: No.

She pulls it back and goes on writing.

DARNLEY: You're cruel, Mary.

MARY: Oh Harry, go away.

DARNLEY: Mary, I'm sorry.

It is touching in its sincerity, pathetic in its infantile inadequacy. She shifts restlessly, and stops writing but doesn't look up, exhaustedly impatient:

MARY: Have you been drinking?

DARNLEY: I'm not drunk.

MARY: You're maudlin.

DARNLEY: It isn't drink that's made me maudlin, as you call it. Not this evening.

He waits. She struggles against it, but:

MARY: What is it then? (*She still hasn't looked up.*)

DARNLEY (*pathetically*): Mary . . .

MARY (*exasperated*): What?

DARNLEY: Look at me.

She blows out an angry sigh, throws down pen and raises her glowering face. But seeing him, her expression alters. She rises, staring, backs away. RIZZIO *and* NAU *come forward alarmed.* DARNLEY *averts his face from them.*

NAU: Your Grace.

MARY: There are sores on his mouth . . . Harry, look at me— What are those sores on your mouth?

Her reaction has appalled him; he rises, stares wildly at RIZZIO *and* NAU *and then defiantly:*

DARNLEY: It's the frost!

MARY: By God, I know that frost—Stand off—! (*He has approached.*)

DARNLEY: Mary—

MARY: Sir, will you not stand off? You are unclean—!

He almost runs to Exit, turns, and in a voice shaking with feeling.

DARNLEY: . . . God save me from a loving woman.

He goes. She starts after him.

MARY: Harry . . . (*She checks.*) Oh Jesus—the child . . . !

RIZZIO *goes to her, alert and calm.*

RIZZIO: When was the child conceived, Maria?

MARY: Four—four and a half months.

RIZZIO: And have you seen the sores before?

MARY: No?

RIZZIO: The child is safe.

MARY: Oh Davie, do you really know?

RIZZIO: Indeed. In Padua this useful branch of knowledge was the most highly regarded of my many accomplishments. I was greatly in demand. But do you know I have never been so greatly in demand as I have since we came to this godly city of Edinburgh? I think it is the cold, you know; it brings people together . . . Ah good, you laugh. And the child is safe.

MARY: Thank God for Davie.

RIZZIO: I do, frequently.

She smiles again, but then her smile fades.

MARY: And . . . him?

RIZZIO: Your husband. Hm. The English have a saying: You have made your bed and you must lie in it. Myself I have never seen the need for this; when there are other beds.

She drifts towards Exit. Turns, looks at him, then softly.

MARY: Davie, bring your lute.

She goes. RIZZIO, *delicately, rising:*

RIZZIO: Aha!

NAU: Signor Rizzio—Don't go to her!

RIZZIO: Oh come, Claud, the Queen needs (*He makes a deliberately ambiguous gesture.*) . . . comfort.

He goes after MARY. NAU *goes separately.* LORDS *enter. Tramp across to table.* MORTON *picks up letter.*

MORTON: Who here has lands from the old Church?

ALL: I.

MORTON: Well you're to lose them.

RUTHVEN: Ach, she hasnae the men.

MORTON: Oh she'll have taken thought for that. It'll be Frenchmen maybe, or maybe mercenaries, but no no she thought of that before she did this. (*Puts it down.*) So what's to do?

RUTHVEN: Fight.

MORTON: It's gey expensive fightin'. An' you can always lose.

RUTHVEN: What then?

From behind the curtain at head of the shallow pyramid of stairs, the sound of the lute, playing RIZZIO'S *tune. They turn and look. Light begins to gather, ominous.*

MORTON: I'm getting to like that instrument. Verra seductive. Aye—a bagpipe's gey stirrin' on the moors but it's no help in a bedroom.

RUTHVEN: What are you talking about?

MORTON: Her husband, you gowk.

LINDSEY: Why what can *he* do?

MORTON: Nothing while he's only that. But suppose he was the

King. And suppose he was bound to us. Bound hard. Our man.

LINDSEY: He's no a man at all.

MORTON: Well call him a man for courtesy. D'you see it?

RUTHVEN: No.

MORTON: Well I do, Ruthven. I see it clear. So either come with me or take yourself off and be damned.

RUTHVEN: I'll come with you.

MORTON: Right, here he is.

    DARNLEY *enters, as before but without the bottle.* MORTON *sotto, urgent:*

Give him a bow, give him a bow.

    They bow. DARNLEY *stops uncertainly.*

DARNLEY: My lords? . . .

MORTON: You look sick, sir. Are you?

DARNLEY: Yes.

MORTON: And so are we, sir, of the same disease.

DARNLEY: What?

MORTON: Domination! Domination by a woman. That we are sick of, and so is Scotland.

DARNLEY: By God you are right, Morton; that is my sickness.

MORTON: We know it, sir. We have watched you. And we think you are too patient. We think the husband of the Queen should be a King.

DARNLEY (*looks at them, breathing hard, pulling at his opened doublet, trying to sober up*): Well?

MORTON: An you would be the King, sir, you must play the leader.

DARNLEY: Leader?

MORTON: Aye. And if you'd be a husband, you must play the man!

    The lute again; a low laugh from MARY.

Ha! They're vigorous enough, heh? They're diligent, heh?

DARNLEY: Wha'—?

MORTON: God's death, my lord, they're going *to* it—now!

DARNLEY: Who—?

MORTON: The monkey—! And your wife!

DARNLEY: *Whaaa*-aa—!

He reels towards the steps, MORTON *grips him by the arm and wheels him round and back. Admiring chuckle.*

MORTON: Did I not say there was a kingly spirit in this man? But see, Your Majesty, these things must be done majestically. I have here a wee paper. Which all of us will sign.

He puts it on the table. Curt nod to his colleagues.

Sign.

As they do:

DARNLEY: What is it?

MORTON: Our warrant.

DARNLEY: Warrant?

MORTON: Aye—or say a promise which we make each to each other, aye and God Almighty too, that what we purpose here is a naething mair nor less than justice for yourself and David Rizzio; nae mair for you, nae less for him. The crown for the King, death for the adulterer. Now you sign.

Thrusts pen into DARNLEY'S *hand.*

DARNLEY: Sign?

MORTON: Kneel, my lairds! (*They kneel.*) This is a solemn moment in the history of Scotland.

Still DARNLEY *hesitates.* MARY'S *low laugh comes again. He turns and looks up at curtain.*

MORTON: They're going to it now, my lord—!—Laughing! Making comparisons!

DARNLEY *whirls back and signs.* LORDS *rise.* MORTON *takes paper, grunts, satisfied, puts it away. He pushes* DARNLEY *aside as done with. All draw daggers.*

Right, my lords. Quick and quiet.

In a swift padding rush they are up the steps, tear down the curtain revealing MARY *and* RIZZIO.

Signor Rizzio!

He grabs RIZZIO, *throws him to the others. They fall on him like a pack of dogs. In the uproar:*

MARY: Ho there! Rescue! Treason! Bothwell! Bothwell!

The mangled corpse is let drop. MARY *falls in shock.* DARNLEY *is hanging off, appalled and nerveless.* MORTON *angry.*

MORTON: Dagger him, man!

DARNLEY *paralyzed. A* LORD *leaps down to him, snatches his dagger, throws it to* MORTON *who plunges it into the corpse.*

A cry of horror from MARY. BOTHWELL *and* NAU *enter at the run. Check as* LORDS *present daggers, crouching.* BOTHWELL *spreads his empty hands, approaches and looks at corpse.*

BOTHWELL: God's death, my lords, you're very thorough. Lord Darnley, I think this is yours.

Tosses dagger to DARNLEY. *He, piteously:*

DARNLEY: Mary, I— . . .

He dashes from the stage.

MORTON: Now Lord Bothwell, are you here to hinder or to help?

BOTHWELL: Neither, Lord Morton.

MORTON: Then you're in my road.

BOTHWELL: Then may I get out of it?

MORTON: Right out of it, Bothwell, out of Edinburgh now.

BOTHWELL: Your Grace. (*She raises her head and looks at him.*) It seems that I must leave you to God's care. I'm for Dunbar. *He goes.*

MORTON: Now Madam, though this was rough yet it was justice.

MARY: No my lord, your pardon, but this was not justice.

She descends unsteadily, NAU *hovering anxiously at her side. She crouches at the corpse and sees the wounds.*

MARY: Oh God . . .

She rises, bewildered.

He was my friend.

MORTON: He was more than that.

MARY: The fault of that was mine. And I ought to have paid for it. (*She sways,* NAU *steps to her.*) Claud, I was born Queen and have proved carnal. I ought to have been born common!

She reaches for support, NAU *catching her and lowering her to the ground.* MORTON *gloomy.*

NAU: Good God, my lord—What have you done?

MORTON: Our duty. Naething more.

Going. LORDS *following he snarls at them:*

Shift it!

MORTON *and* LORDS *go, dragging corpse.* MARY *watches covertly. When they have gone.*

MARY: Morton, Ruthven, Lindsey, Douglas, Glencairn, Falconside and Kerr—

NAU (*startled*): Madam—?

MARY: Remember them! . . . Remind me every day that they must die.

NAU: Oh Madam, this is wild—!—The castle is full of their men!

She looks about. Rises from her knees.

MARY: So we must quit it.

NAU: There is a guard on every door!

MARY: There will be no guard on the kitchen door. Come.

He follows her, shaken, bewildered.

NAU: But Madam, where?

MARY: Where? To the Border—Dunbar!

They go.

CURTAIN

ACT TWO

The throne is on top of the pyramid now. At the foot of the pyramid stands an ornate golden casket three feet high, with carrying handles. KNOX *in pulpit.* MORTON, RUTHVEN, LINDSEY, *gloomy.*

KNOX: Lord, Lord, what tribulations we have seen. What marching, counter-marching, lying down in the wet heather, rising in the night, what ambushes, what wounds, what death . . . (*Plaintively, descending.*) The execution of the adulterer Rizzio was a very Godly deed; you might have thought that it would prosper. But no, no, Man proposes, God disposes, (*bitterly*) Aye, and the Devil looks after his own. This, an't please you, is a Christening font. Aye—it's no an ornament from a brothel, it's a Christening font. Gurnia, gurnia, solid gold.

VOICE OFF: Ho there, the Queen!

MORTON: Now for God's sake, Master Knox, an you must speak, speak small. For our cart has no wheels and the woman's rampant.

Enter ELIZABETH, WALSINGHAM, LEICESTER, CECIL.

ELIZABETH: Are these the murderers?

KNOX: There was no murder, Madam.

ELIZABETH: What then?

KNOX: Godly execution.

ELIZABETH: I do not think I know a Godly execution. But I know the difference between execution and murder—It is the Royal Warrant.

MORTON: We had it, Madam.

ELIZABETH (*to* WALSINGHAM, *contemptuous*): Darnley's 'warrant'.

KNOX: No Madam, God's.

53

ELIZABETH: Oh—did he sign it too?

KNOX: That's verra blasph—

ELIZABETH: Peace, Master Knox. We are no Edinburgh house-
wife. Morton, how came the Queen to escape?

MORTON: She spoke me fair, Madam—God help me, she seemed
(*indignantly*) remorseful.

ELIZABETH: You mean she fooled you.

MORTON: Your Grace, the woman is a verra serpent!

ELIZABETH: Poor Adam. Poor, thick-witted, bloody-handed,
Scottish Adam. What do you expect of me?

MORTON: Your mercy, Madam.

KNOX: And your aid, Madam.

ELIZABETH: For our mercy, it is universal and you have it. For
our aid: we tell you here before the world, we aid no rebels.
For royalty and rebellion, both are indivisible. Go.

　　They go.

Walsingham. Give them money.

WALSINGHAM: Yes, Your Grace. How much?

ELIZABETH: As little as will keep them rebellious. Cecil, talk
to Lord Morton.

CECIL: Your Grace.

ELIZABETH: Robin, you have the hardest task.

DUDLEY: Your Grace?

ELIZABETH: Listen to Master Knox. Now—leave us.

　　*They go. She approaches the font and looks at it carefully. To
　　herself:*

She escapes . . . down little stairs and greasy passages, she
escapes, through the kitchens. I do not know where the
kitchens are . . . And then in the dark, in the sweet smelling
stables, she saddles her own horse; he knows her, he is quiet . . .
I cannot saddle a horse. And then she rides, down rocky screes,
through mountain rivers, two days and nights two hundred
miles, she must have ridden without sleep . . . And I am
sleepless; I am spent. And then, this Bothwell—raises men,
half-naked men whose whole wealth is a sword, and drives

her enemies from Edinburgh—and for what? Why, for herself . . . And now she returns, but easily now, easily. (*Harsh.*)
For she is big with child. And that child is my heir, for I am
a barren stock!

She ascends to throne as MARY, LADIES, BOTHWELL,
ARCHBISHOP, MOR *and* NAU *enter.* MARY *carrying a baby. She
goes to the font.* ELIZABETH *calls:*

Your Grace—Your rebel subjects came here and appealed to
us. But we have given them a sour reply. And for a further
token of our love, we send you this.

MARY: Your Grace, we guess what manner of reply you gave
our rebel subjects. Your Grace may guess our gratitude. And
for this further token of your love—Why, we will put it to
good use!

ARCHBISHOP *dips into font and:*

ARCHBISHOP: In the name of the Father, Son, and Holy Ghost:
James Stuart, Prince of Scotland, Ireland, and England!

Fanfare.

ELIZABETH *exits above.*

MARY *takes the child, peering at it delightedly, taking it back
towards* BOTHWELL, *softly:*

MARY: Hey boy, shall we ride? Hey? Shall we ride together you
and I—Hey boy? Shall we then—?—Oh! (*She laughs up at*
BOTHWELL.) *He sneezed!*

BOTHWELL *nods coldly and:*

BOTHWELL: He's very talented, no doubt about it.

MARY *smiles, says again to the baby:*

MARY: And so he is. No doubt about it.

NAU: Your Grace must now appoint the Lord Protector.

BOTHWELL: The job is spoken for.

MARY: What needs he with a Lord Protector? He will make
shift with a Queen Protector—Won't you boy, hey?

NAU: Madam, these are not the times to break an ancient custom;
beseech you to decide upon some valiant and sober gentleman
who—

BOTHWELL: Are you deaf, man—?—The job's spoken for.

 MARY *looks at* BOTHWELL *thoughtfully, a little sadly, down again at the baby and softly:*

MARY: Lord Mar.

 MAR *steps forward.* BOTHWELL *watches darkly.*

Lord Mar, I give into your guard this most precious burden.

MAR: It is a trust that I will answer for to God himself, Your Grace.

MARY (*smiling, ready to weep, relinquishing the baby*): Thanks, my lord.

 MAR *goes with baby,* LADIES *following.* MARY'S *eyes and body yearn after them and:*

Bring him to me, ladies, before supper!

 All go except MARY *and* BOTHWELL.

BOTHWELL (*quietly*): So you don't trust me.

MARY (*frightened, placating*): With myself I trust you.

 Looking away from her, gloomily grunts.

BOTHWELL: Mebbe.

MARY: I have no choice but trust you, being your slave.

BOTHWELL: Don't you know yourself better than that? You're nobody's slave.

MARY: It is you who do not know me. See.

 She goes down, clasping his legs, abased.

BOTHWELL: That's just extravagance. Let go my legs. You want it both ways, Mary. Like—you'll feed me food on a fork. But I must eat it whether I've a mind to it or not, or you'll sling the plate across the room. You've a bluidy awful temper, d'you know that?

MARY: Yes.

BOTHWELL: An you were my wife, I'd have taken a whip to you before this.

MARY: Well, I would be your wife in anything I can.

 She smiles up sideways and catlike, but he leaves her; soberly:

BOTHWELL: I doubt that. With me to your bed here in Edinburgh, and Darnley to your husband away there in Glasgow,

you have it both ways, the way you want it. I doubt you'd
be my wife.

MARY: I have given you no cause to doubt it.

BOTHWELL: There's an easy way to prove it. Fetch him
here.

She rises, wretched, looks away.

He, sadly, bitterly:

You're playing, Mary. You play at everything. You think
that life's a game and you the only one allowed to cheat.
Well it's no a game and you canna cheat, for there are no rules.
It's real. But you're no a real woman.

MARY: You lie.

BOTHWELL: Yes I lie. Come here.

*She goes to him. He kisses her, quite gently. Her response
becomes fierce. Deliberately, he holds her away and:*

Do you fetch him?

She searches his face.

MARY: Jamie, do you know what you are asking?

BOTHWELL: Yes; everything. Ought I to ask for less?

MARY: I'll fetch him.

She goes. BOTHWELL *calls:*

BOTHWELL: Ormiston!

ORMISTON *enters, peeling an apple.*

Well?

ORMISTON: Well . . . I have forty-five pounds of it; in three wee
kegs. It should suffice.

BOTHWELL: To Hell with should; will it?

ORMISTON: It's no just the verra best powder I've seen; it has
a sort of greyish look—guid powder's black. And Kirk o'
Field's a gey strong house. Aye, strongly built. What like did
you want with the house?

BOTHWELL: I want it lifted off the earth.

ORMISTON: Forty-five pounds'll no do that.

BOTHWELL: Get more then.

ORMISTON: That's a' verra well. It's not easy come by, not

quietly. And there's enough folk ken what you're about
already.

BOTHWELL: Who?

ORMISTON: That's hard to say. But since she went to Glasgow
there's been a sort of gathering in the air. Have you not
noticed?

BOTHWELL: Yes.

   TALA *enters with letter. Gives it to* BOTHWELL.

TALA: A letter, laird, from herself in Glasgow.

BOTHWELL: How is it?

TALA: You're in deep water I would say. He's awfu' sick. She's
sorry for him.

BOTHWELL: Hell!

   *He opens the letter and reads. The two men look over his
shoulder.*

ORMISTON: It's a guid hand is that.

TALA: It's a French hand.

ORMISTON: Is that right?

BOTHWELL: Off, you dogs!

   He reads:

   'Being absent from him who has my heart—' mp.

   Turns several pages impatiently.

TALA: It's a long letter.

ORMISTON: Why wouldn't it be? It's a love letter.

BOTHWELL: 'His sickness abates yet he has almost slain me with
his breath though I came no nearer than the bed's foot. For
Rizzio he says—' Curse what he says, is he coming? 'Alas my
lord—' (*Impatient growl, another page.*) 'I cannot sleep because
I cannot sleep . . .' Hell and Damnation is he coming or not?
'Summa. He will not come except— . . . And so I have
promised. We come—

   He turns a page. Breathes out, satisfied:

to-morrow . . .' Ormiston, how much to make it certain?

ORMISTON: Another hundred pounds.

BOTHWELL: Get it from the armoury.

Throws a ring of keys which ORMISTON *catches and, dangling them, dubiously.*

ORMISTON: It's awfu' obvious.

BOTHWELL (*scanning letter again*): Do it.

ORMISTON: You're the master; I'm the man.

He goes, with TALA. BOTHWELL *reads again:*

BOTHWELL: 'It is late, I am alone, I desire never to cease writing, yet now must cease for lack of paper and so end my letter. Read it twice or thrice. Burn it.' Burn it? Oh no, my love; this is my warrant.

MARY *enters above. She is alone.*

Fierce:

Where is he? Have you not fetched him?

MARY: Yes. Jamie, what do you mean to do?

He looks at her hard.

BOTHWELL: Don't ask what I will do. You've done your part.

DARNLEY *and* DOCTOR *enter above.* DARNLEY *wears a weird white mask, white gloves and slippers, a fanciful white dressing gown.*

DARNLEY: Mary—

BOTHWELL *turns and stares.*

BOTHWELL: What—?

MARY: Jamie—He is defaced.

BOTHWELL: Defaced— ?—Why it's only a touch of the pox, my Lord. Let's have a look—

MARY: Leave him alone, Jamie!

He turns and stares at her grimly.

DARNLEY: Bothwell—The Queen and I are reconciled.

BOTHWELL: Yes I see you are . . . (*Turns back to* DARNLEY *cheerful.*) And I'm very glad of it, my Lord. I have your room prepared at Kirk o' Field.

DARNLEY: What, am I not for the castle?

BOTHWELL: The Doctors say the air at Kirk o' Fields is healthier. Is that not right, Doctor?

DOCTOR: The air at Kirk o' Fields, Lord Bothwell, is humorous, the place being—

BOTHWELL: —My Doctor says its healthier. (*Cheerful again to* DARNLEY.) And we've everything made ready there. But we can shift you to the castle in the morning if you like.

   During this MARY, *staring at* BOTHWELL, *has come to stand protectively near* DARNLEY, *behind his chair.*

DARNLEY: Well . . . (*To* MARY.) Will you come with me?

MARY (*looking over his head at* BOTHWELL *defiantly*): Yes.

BOTHWELL: Well you cannot go tonight, Your Grace. The Dance is tonight.

MARY: The dance?

BOTHWELL: Your guid friend Bastien's—

   Unseen by DARNLEY *he jabs his thumb at his own chest, identifying 'Bastien'—*

wedding dance.

MARY: I will excuse myself.

BOTHWELL: Well you can do that if you like—But I fancy it's the last you'll see of Bastien, if you do.

MARY: I will come to you, Harry, after the dance!

BOTHWELL: Kirk o' Fields, Doctor! Good-night, my lord.

DARNLEY (*going*): Mary . . .?

MARY: I will come to you, Harry, after the dance!

   DARNLEY *and* DOCTOR *gone.*

   Dully again:

Is it tonight?

BOTHWELL: Is what tonight?

MARY: I do not know.

BOTHWELL (*gently*): That's right. So dance.

   MUSIC. *He takes her hand. They dance the Pavane. Lights fade. Shadowy figures enter behind, dancing two by two.* MARY *in bright spot, puppetlike under* BOTHWELL'S *compelling stare. He leaves her. She makes an involuntary gesture to retain him. Then dances on alone, her face frightened.* MUSIC *ceases. A solitary drum taps out the time. Then on Speakers a Child's Voice:*

CHILD'S VOICE (*speaker*): 'Mary, Mary, quite contrary, how

does your garden grow? With silver bells and cockle shells
and pretty maids—'

*The stage rocks in blinding light. A distant explosion bellows.
Uproar, Dancers scattering, bells and crowd roaring on Speaker.*
KNOX *dashes on, beside himself, stands in the spot vacated by*
MARY.

KNOX: Did I not warn you? Did I not say? Did I not prophesy?
Was not the very face of Heaven dark the day she set her foot
on Scottish soil?

Lights   up.   The   Dancers   revealed   as   ELIZABETH,
WALSINGHAM, CECIL; LADIES, DE QUADRA, PHILIP;
POPE *and* PRIEST. *The* SCOTS LORDS *are on the lowest step of
pyramid, looking up like everybody else at* MARY *seated on throne,*
BOTHWELL *by her, both composed but desperately tense.*

How long, guid people of Edinburgh—how long? Are you
God's children and the nurslings of the Kirk and will you have
a bloody handed strumpet for your Queen?

MARY: John Knox—you are a traitor and a—

BOTHWELL: —Hold hard, the world is watching you.

MARY: Good Master Knox, we have no quarrel with you—or
our people.

KNOX: By Heaven, we have a quarrel with you!

ELIZABETH: Your Grace, we should not do the office of a
cousin and a friend unless we urged Your Grace to clear yourself. Repudiate that man—bring him to trial!

MARY: We thank Your Grace, but this gentleman has stood his
trial and is found innocent.

KNOX: We know the manner of that trial, and if he's innocent,
why so is Satan!

MARY: The law stands over all of us, and we think as the law
does, that the gentleman is innocent. In proof of which know
all the world that we are married.

KNOX: That does not prove his innocence—it indicates your guilt!

POPE: A Protestant pantomime, my child, no marriage. Repudiate him.

MARY: Your Holiness, although the form was empty yet our hearts were in it; I account us married in the eyes of God.

PHILIP: Poor fool, poor *fool*!

KNOX: Oh my! What sympathy these Catholics show for their own kind. The King of Spain now. Thinks himself a verra pious man. The ladies of his Court must dress just so, no hanky-panky in the Prado no, a verra nunnery they say. Well here we have adultery, and bigamy, and murder—! And what says His pious Majesty? Why not a word.

PHILIP: We nothing doubt but that the lady was involved against her will and merits leniency.

KNOX: The woman is a common criminal and merits death.

The Dancers wheel, look up at MARY, *go.*

MARY: Lord Mar—Give me my child.

She half descends to meet MAR *who moves to meet her, but* MORTON:

MORTON: Give her the child, you give it to Lord Bothwell, Mar. Is that how you'll discharge your trust?

MAR hesitates.

MARY: Lord Mar—!

MAR: I cannot, Madam, while that man is by your side.

MORTON: So let us have Lord Bothwell and you can have your child.

MARY: What mean you with Lord Bothwell?

MORTON: We mean to hang him.

MARY (*kisses her fingertips and tenderly extends her arm towards her child*): Farewell, child . . .

MAR goes and she watches him off. BOTHWELL *grins at* MORTON.

MORTON: You're makin' it hard for us, Your Grace, but you're makin' it gey harder for yourself. To me, Bothwell. (He *and* LORDS *draw their daggers.*)

BOTHWELL: Ormiston!

MORTON: We've hanged him already.

BOTHWELL: Tala! Bowton! A Hepburn! A Hepburn!

MORTON: You're wasting your breath, man—you have a sort of plague. Are you coming down or must we come up?

BOTHWELL draws his dagger. MORTON *sighs.*

Verra well, my lords—Quick and quiet.

LORDS start for the steps.

MARY: Stop!

They stop.

Lord Morton, if I submit myself to you, will you let Lord Bothwell go?

MORTON (*considers, nods, pleased*): . . . Done.

LORDS protest.

Peace, you fools. What's one Border Bandit more or less? Bothwell, you have three days to quit Scotland.

MARY: Go, Jamie.

He kisses her, is going.

Be true!

BOTHWELL: I only met one woman in my life; d'you think I'll no come back for her?

He goes. She looking after him, radiant. Turns to MORTON,

MARY: Now may you do your worst, Lord Morton.

MORTON: Well I ask myself what I am to do with you.

His tone is quite friendly, and KNOX, *alert and threatening:*

KNOX: Morton, will you parley with this harlot?

MORTON: I will, John. Yes.

KNOX: Then I will go and parley with the People!

They measure glances.

MORTON: You do that, John.

He watches KNOX *exit then sighs.*

Gurnia, gurnia, troubled times . . . The way of it, Your Grace is this: We cannot and we will not have Lord Bothwell for our King. You must see that? But neither would we have the People for our King. A Queen, you see, is a great convenience to the nobility—And vicky versa. Now, you're not tied to Bothwell very hard. The way I see it, that marriage was no marriage. Because, the way I see it, you was forced. So you

see, Your Grace, if you'll just say that you was forced,
repudiate the man, why then, we're all in step again.

MARY: And what if I refuse?

MORTON: Now what would you gain by that? He'll no come
back.

MARY: He will come back.

MORTON: If he comes back we'll put him to the horn and hunt
him down like any other outlaw and he knows it. There's no
'Chivalry' in Bothwell.

MARY: Still you have not told me what, if I refuse.

MORTON: Prison. And I do not mean 'confinement' in some
bra' house, no no—I mean a Highland keep. I mean one small,
strong, room, for the rest of your days. And you're young yet.

MARY: And that is my choice?

MORTON: It is, d'you want time to think?

MARY: No. For prison, I will quit it. And then woe to you;
woe to this country. For Lord Bothwell . . .

Her level voice falters on it. Then strongly.

My lords, I would follow him to the edge of the earth—in my
shift!

MORTON (*angry*): . . . You obdurate shrew. Awa' wi' her!

He shoves her into their arms. They run her off stage, MORTON
looking after. Light change. Enter ELIZABETH, WALSINGHAM,
CECIL.

ELIZABETH: To the edge of the earth . . .?

MORTON: Aye, Your Grace. In her shift.

ELIZABETH: . . . Well . . . Where is she?

MORTON (*complacent*): We have her fast. (*Grim satisfaction.*) At
Loch Leven.

ELIZABETH: What is that?

MORTON: A Highland keep, Your Grace; the keep on an island,
the island in a lake.

ELIZABETH: Her jailer?

MORTON (*chuckle*): Dinna fash about that, Your Grace. He'd as
soon break her neck as look at her. Black Douglas is his name.

ELIZABETH: Who has the child?

MORTON (*sour smile*): One George Buchanan, a verra Godly friend of Master Knox.

ELIZABETH (*nods*): Will the Queen see the child?

MORTON: She will not.

ELIZABETH: Well. Rule Scotland wisely, Morton, till the little King grows up.

She pushes a bag of coins across the table. MORTON, *unctuously:*

MORTON: I will rule as Your Grace would wish.

Enter DAVISON.

DAVISON: Your pardon, Your Grace. Master Cecil, this presses. (*Gives letter to* CECIL.) From the Border, Your Grace. It concerns Lord Morton somewhat.

MORTON: Me?

CECIL (*eyes on the paper*): Yes . . . Yes, rather more than somewhat. The Queen of Scots is free, Your Grace.

ELIZABETH: Free?

CECIL: Yes, Your Grace, it—

MORTON: I dinna believe it!

CECIL (*still scanning paper*): It would appear that your mysoginistic friend Black Douglas has a son, of a more impressionable temper.

MORTON: What—! (*Snatches letter and peruses it, breathing hard.*) ELIZABETH *laughs suddenly.* CECIL *goes on:*

CECIL: And the keep had a window. And the lake had a boat. ELIZABETH *laughs again.* MORTON *looks up.*

MORTON: What Madam, are you merry?

ELIZABETH: All men are merry for a moment, Morton, to see a bird go free. There, my merriment is over.

MORTON: I think so, Madam. She is in England.

CECIL: What?

MORTON (*cheerfully*): Aye—She's in Carlisle, Master Cecil, lodged with the Earl of Westmorland—

WALSINGHAM (*alarmed, to* CECIL):—Westmorland!

MORTON: Aye—And other Catholic gentlemen are flocking

there—'flocking' that's the word here. To cap it a', she throws herself on Your Grace's mercy and (*throws down the letter*) asks audience.

ELIZABETH *picks up the letter and stares at it. Then, almost to herself, in a voice almost of dread:*

ELIZABETH: Why me . . .? Why my mercy . . .? We are enemies.

CECIL *is watching her carefully; now, carefully:*

CECIL: If you see her, Your Grace, you will seem to condone the murder of Lord Darnley.

WALSINGHAM: That woman alive in England is a Trojan Horse. Execute her!

ELIZABETH: It would not be seen as the execution of a murderess, good Francis, it would be seen as the elimination of a rival.

CECIL: Yes . . . It would *be* the elimination of a rival, of course.

ELIZABETH: No.

CECIL: I wonder if the matter is not Scottish domestic . . .

ELIZABETH: Good . . . (*Smiling.*) Lord Morton, you may take our sister back to Scotland and (*Smile goes flat and expressionless.*) do with her what you will.

MORTON (*reproving grin*): Oh no, Your Grace. She's yours. An' Your Grace is welcome. (*Takes money, going.*) Where she is, there is no safety.

He goes. They look after him.

WALSINGHAM: There is no safety for Your Grace's person *while* she is. She has connived at murder once and will again.

CECIL: I would that we had proof that she connived at it.

WALSINGHAM: I have a letter here, would hang her in a common court. She wrote it from Glasgow. It was taken from among Lord Bothwell's papers.

ELIZABETH *takes it; is troubled; thrusts it at* CECIL *who takes it eagerly and then asks with mild curiosity.*

CECIL: Is it genuine, Master Walsingham, or forged?

WALSINGHAM: Read it.

ELIZABETH: Aloud.

CECIL (*reads*): 'Being absent from the place where I left my heart, I was like a body without a heart—'

    ELIZABETH shifts fractionally. CECIL *registers it, says to* WALSINGHAM.

Poetic; hardly proof.

WALSINGHAM: Read the portions I have marked.

CECIL (*reads*): 'Alas my lord, you have sent me here to do a work I much detest . . .' er '. . . Certainly he fears the thing you know of and for his life. But I had but to speak two or three kind words and he was happy. Then he showed so many little courtesies so seriously and wisely that you would be amazed. Alas, alas, and I never deceived anybody . . .' er 'It is late and yet I cannot sleep because I cannot sleep as I desire, that is in your arms, my dear life . . .'

    She shifts again. He stops, lays down the letter.

More of the like.

ELIZABETH: Finish it.

CECIL: Madam, the rest is—(*Waves the rest away.*)

ELIZABETH: Finish it.

    He picks it up and reads the rest in a tone which tries to drain it of emotion and therefore heightens it:

CECIL: 'Now God forgive me and God give you, my only love, the fortune which your humble faithful love desires for you. It is late. I am alone. I desire never to cease writing to you, yet now must cease for lack of paper. And so I kiss your hands and end my letter. Read it twice or thrice. Burn it.'

    He lays it down, and waits for her response. It comes flatly:

ELIZABETH: And he kept it.

WALSINGHAM: Happily, Madam, yes.

ELIZABETH: Well that is no forgery. (*She rises, not looking at them.*) Send sufficient force and bring her as far South as Sheffield Castle. Confine her there. But as a Queen.

WALSINGHAM: She may correspond?

ELIZABETH: She may do anything a Queen may do. Except leave Sheffield Castle.

WALSINGHAM: It is not wise, Your Grace.

ELIZABETH: It is our will! (*Turns at exit to say unconvincingly.*) We fear the French connection.

She goes. WALSINGHAM *severe:*

WALSINGHAM: Her Grace is too merciful!

CECIL: I do not think that this is altogether mercy. I think our Queen sees Mary in the mirror.

WALSINGHAM: You are grown so subtle, Master Cecil, you will shortly be invisible.

He goes, impatient, CECIL *following. Light change. Enter separately,* NAU *and* SERVANT *who puts down a small keg.*

SERVANT: There sir, from Lord Shrewsbury's own hopyards. The best beer in England.

NAU: Lord Shrewsbury is a kindly jailer. Thank him.

SERVANT goes. MARY *enters slowly, in a simple riding habit, carrying a whip.*

Where did you ride, Your Grace?

MARY: To the North Gate, Claud.

She somnambulates past him. Stops.

And then to the West Gate . . . And so to the South Gate . . . And back to the Castle.

NAU: Are you unwell?

MARY: I am in the best health possible, for prison. This morning I am cured of hope.

NAU: Madam?

MARY: I met a person in the Park. A Catholic gentleman. He said 'God Bless Your Grace'. And gave me news of my lord Bothwell. He will not come back, Claud. He is in Denmark.

NAU: Perhaps he waits his time, Your Grace.

MARY: He has taken service with the King of Denmark.

NAU: He must provide for himself somehow.

MARY: He has bought a house.

NAU: He must have a roof.

MARY: There is a lady in the house.

NAU: How did the gentleman know all this?

MARY: He has seen it.

   NAU *has no answer, looks at her in pity. She gives him a pale smile.*

   He only told me what you told me long ago. And what my own heart has been heavy with these twelve slow months. I think the months will seem to pass more swiftly now. (*She looks at him.*) Claud, I do not ask that you should share them.

NAU: An't please Your Grace, I will share them.

MARY: Henceforth you are the only man that I will trust. (*Bitter self-recrimination.*) Besides the man I ought to have staked my life on from the start.

NAU: What man is that, Your Grace?

MARY: The little man in Scotland, Claud.

NAU: It is cruel that they do not let you see him.

MARY: I see him every night. We talk before we sleep.

NAU: What does he say?

MARY: That he loves me right well. And forgives me . . . And, that when he is of age, he will come out of Scotland like a second Tamurlaine—!—With bloody punishment in either hand for these water hearted beerdrinkers!

NAU: Oh Madam, be patient!

MARY: Well, I will.

NAU: You must, Your Grace!

MARY: I must.

   She has made a swift tour of the stage, mindless as an animal and comes now to a halt with her whip flicking restlessly. NAU *looks at her uneasily; a silence, then, indicating the keg at his feet he offers:*

NAU (*cheerfully*): Myself, I have learned to *like* the beer.

MARY: It is an accomplishment.

   The whip flicks again. He eyes her again.

NAU: Show patient, Madam, and the English may at length show kind.

MARY: By God, they'll show unlike themselves then.

NAU: There is kindness in the circumstances they allow you

here. And Mignon, you would need less patience if you would make more use of them.

MARY: I use the Park. (*She shows him the whip.*)

NAU: Your riding to and fro like one demented half the day serves but to remind you that the Park has walls. There is a wide world in the library.

MARY: I'll come more often to the library.

NAU: There are some fine romances there.

MARY (*a pause*): I have done with romances. (*A pause.*) Henceforth I'll study policy.

NAU: Patience now is your only policy.

MARY: No.

NAU: What other?

MARY: Claud, this gentleman whom I met riding in the Park. He will carry letters, secret letters; they will not be overlooked.

NAU: Oh no—!

MARY: He is waiting for me now.

NAU: Waiting for—?—Oh Madam, Madam—What do you know of this gentleman—?—Think! Your life lies every morning in the Queen of England's hand.

MARY: She does not dare.

NAU: And if you give her just occasion she will dare! Be patient! and *preserve* yourself!

She considers it. Then, reasonably, quietly:

MARY: For what?

NAU: For quietness. Your Grace, you have some need of quietness. In quietness we save our souls.

MARY: Sir, do you think I do not know what state my soul is in . . .?

It rebukes him.

But listen now. God gives each one of us a different life to live. And if we live it well he gives us everlasting life in Heaven. And if we live it ill, as surely I have lived right ill, yet still may Heaven be merciful. But if we live it not at all nay then I think Heaven has no mercy—And God made me a

Queen! I did not beg to be so born. And maybe I was not equipped to be so born. But since I was so born—(*She collects herself.*)—By Heaven I will so live!

She goes where she entered, but striding fast. NAU *separately. An echoing cry of anguish, off:*

VOICE OFF: No—no—no—no—! (*A pause.*) Oh God—!—Help me!

PRISONER *dragged into spot by* JAILERS. CECIL *and* WALSINGHAM *enter as lights come up.*

They do not look. WALSINGHAM *sits.* CECIL *addresses audience.*

CECIL: The Pope of Rome is a dangerous simpleton. And he has had letters from the Queen of Scots which I fear dangerously misrepresent the situation here. For here I have his Papal edict 'Regnans in Excelsis' which releases English Catholics from allegiance to the Queen. Nay more—It makes it meritorious in English Catholics to assassinate the Queen. And more again—It calls for a crusade to invade the territories of the Queen. So now our English Catholics have to choose, between his Holiness and her Majesty. Well His Holiness is far away and Her Majesty is close at hand and we her Ministers are (*half glance at* PRISONER) busy. How would you choose? Yes, and so do most of them. Not all, though . . . No, not all. (*He joins* WALSINGHAM *at table.*) Well, I see that you have racked him.

JAILER: Yes, sir.

CECIL: Can he stand?

JAILER: No, sir.

CECIL: A chair then.

PRISONER *seated.* CECIL *looks at him unwillingly. His silvery old man's voice is courteous, dispassionate and fatal:*

CECIL: Now sir, again, who are you?

PRISONER: I am Nicholas Benson. Cloth Merchant, of Amsterdam.

CECIL: No sir. You are—

WALSINGHAM *gives him paper.*

—Father Edward Fenton and you are a Jesuit priest. You were trained at Douai and sent here from there. While you were in prison at Norwich you administered the Sacrament of 'absolution' to a man you took to be a fellow prisoner awaiting death. And you told him all this. One Peter Blunt.

PRISONER: Oh . . . Was Peter not a prisoner?

CECIL: No. he was an instrument of Master Walsingham's.

PRISONER: Oh. (*Without much feeling.*) I am undone then.

CECIL: Yes. Now, your letters—(*Reaching for them.*)

PRISONER: They are not my letters.

CECIL: The letters which were found beneath the floorboards of your room. They implicate you in a plot, which we already know about. (*Gently, pleadingly.*) We know about it, sir.

PRISONER: What need to question then?

CECIL: I should like to understand you if I could. Did you know that your associates intended to assassinate Her Majesty?

No answer.

Did you know that following that, one hundred Catholic gentlemen would seize the port of Norwich while two thousand Spanish troops were landed there—on English soil?

WALSINGHAM: To make that bloody-handed harlot Mary Stuart, England's Queen? And do you call this a Crusade? And yourself English?

PRISONER: God made Mary Stuart England's Queen. It is not for me—or you—to question it.

WALSINGHAM: Ho! 'God' quotha! Lackaday! what Christianity is this!

CECIL: Walsingham. Look sir, you know that you must die—

PRISONER: I do; and God be thanked am ready to.

CECIL: I see you are. But you can die by burning, as a priest. Or, for treason, quickly by the axe. That choice I can give you . . . Now. I want to know if Mary Stuart instigated, or approved, or knew about your plans . . . Sir, I have seen death by burning, in Mary Tudor's time. I know which I would choose.

PRISONER (*smiles faintly*): But then I have a higher calling than yourself. I am a priest. And I will die as one.

A beat.

Then CECIL *motions with his hand and* JAILERS *remove* PRISONER. CECIL'S *face is pinched and wrinkled with distaste. He tells the audience:*

CECIL: One grows old quickly at this work.

ELIZABETH *enters. She too is older than before. Her face, framed in an extravagantly flaring collar, is more obviously painted. She growls suspiciously at* CECIL.

ELIZABETH: What do you say, Cecil?

CECIL: That I am growing old, Your Grace. It is only Your Grace who has the secret of eternal youth, and shines on like the morning star when all the rest have fled, a rainbow among clouds, a rose in Winter.

ELIZABETH: Leave flattery to courtiers. You give good measure but the quality is coarse. Well; what have you found?

WALSINGHAM: We have found the same as always, Madam: Mary Stuart. Mary Stuart and Catholic Conspiracy, Mary Stuart and a Spanish rescue, Mary Stuart and Your Grace's death. Your Grace was to have been shot down with muskets in the knot garden at Hampton Court, on Tuesday next.

ELIZABETH: Muskets? In the knot garden . . .? God's death, how long does this go on?

WALSINGHAM: As long as Mary Stuart lives, Your Grace.

ELIZABETH: Have you proof of her complicity?

WALSINGHAM: No proof, Your Grace, but no doubt either.

ELIZABETH: I will not do it without proof.

She says it stubbornly, as something said before, and WALSINGHAM *looks at* CECIL *who:*

CECIL: Your Grace, there is news from Spain. The Duke of Parma is appointed to command the Spanish armies in the Netherlands.

Enter DAVISON.

DAVISON: Your Grace, the Spanish Ambassador asks instant audience.

ELIZABETH: Tomorrow.

Exit DAVISON.

Parma for the Netherlands.

CECIL: Yes, Your Grace. He will be followed by fifty thousand infantry.

ELIZABETH: Oh . . . This is not for the Netherlands.

WALSINGHAM: No, Your Grace, it is for us. And it will find the country in two minds—because it has two Queens!

ELIZABETH: I cannot do it without proof!

WALSINGHAM goes. She rises: energy beginning to flow from her visibly.

Yet, Parma. Something I must do.

CECIL: Yes, Your Grace.

ELIZABETH: What?

CECIL: May I speak without fear?

ELIZABETH: I do not know that; you may speak.

CECIL: Recall the Earl of Leicester.

ELIZABETH: Nay, you had done better to be silent.

CECIL: Your Grace, he is a soldier.

ELIZABETH: I have other soldiers.

CECIL: But none so fit.

ELIZABETH: Fit—? An he were Hannibal he were not fit— He is treacherous!

CECIL: Madam, marriage is not treachery.

ELIZABETH: But secrecy is treachery! Speak no more of Leicester, he is ruined! What—Ten months the slippery villain plays it out with 'Yes, Your Grace' and 'No, Your Grace' and then 'A trifle I would tell Your Grace—I am married these ten months'! Speak not, Cecil—!—I will not hear!

CECIL: Or let me speak or let me go, Your Grace.

ELIZABETH: Nay, go then.

He goes.

Come back.

He comes back.

Suffolk?

CECIL: Too old, Your Grace.

ELIZABETH: Mountjoy?

CECIL: Too young.

She goes to throne, calls formally:

ELIZABETH: Recall the Earl—of Leicester!

Enter DAVISON *and* DUDLEY, *also older than before.*

My lord.

He kisses her hand and rises.

Are you well?

DUDLEY: Well indeed, Your Grace. Now.

ELIZABETH: And your wife?

DUDLEY: Well too, Your Grace.

ELIZABETH: You are happy?

DUDLEY: I am a husband, Madam.

ELIZABETH: You make it sound little. What more would you be?

She is looking away. DUDLEY *snatches a look at* CECIL, *who nods.*

DUDLEY: Your Grace—this summer—I hope to be a father.

She looks at him. Moves; right past him to table.

ELIZABETH: Take your place, my lord.

CECIL: My lord is acquainted with the occasion.

She returns from her abstraction.

ELIZABETH: Oh yes, the occasion. What do you think?

DUDLEY: I think we might shock them, if we had time to muster, and if the country were united.

ELIZABETH: . . . And what do you think might unite the country?

DUDLEY: The death of Mary Stuart.

ELIZABETH (*softly*): By God, time was you had other plans for Mary Stuart.

DUDLEY (*uncomfortable*): Time has changed, Your Grace.

ELIZABETH: And you with it. I hope you will prove a constant
  soldier, Robin; for Heaven knows you're an unsteady swain.
  Silence. She throws it off. Brisk:
  How long to muster?

DUDLEY: Three to muster, three to train.

ELIZABETH: Six months in all. And Parma's veterans have not
  been out of iron for sixteen years—And he will shock them.
  Cecil, this fifty thousand—will they come overland?
  *She sits bolt upright and expressionless during what follows, a
  political computer gathering information.*

CECIL: They will if France will let them through, Your Grace.

ELIZABETH: And will France let them through?

CECIL: Not if Your Grace will make the French alliance.

ELIZABETH: Meaning the French marriage.

CECIL: Yes, Your Grace.

ELIZABETH: Walsingham, has Spain sufficient ships to carry
  fifty thousand?

WALSINGHAM: Your Grace, there is such hammering in the
  Spanish shipyards that Spain shakes.

ELIZABETH: Have we sufficient ships to sink them?

CECIL: Not yet, Your Grace.

ELIZABETH: And you require six months to muster.

DUDLEY: Yes, Your Grace.

  CLERK *enters.*

CLERK: Señor de Quadra, as Your Grace appointed yesterday,
  asks audience again today.

ELIZABETH: Again tomorrow.

  CLERK *goes. She turns to* DAVISON.
  You sir, tell the French Prince we will have him.

  DAVISON *goes.*

WALSINGHAM: He is a Catholic, Your Grace; your people will
  not have him.

ELIZABETH: Nor will we; so send a hundred thousand crowns
  to him, to keep his relish for our person keen.

  WALSINGHAM *goes, while* CECIL *gasps:*

CECIL: A hundred thousand crowns, Your Grace!

ELIZABETH: Our person needs a little spice. Sell Crown lands to the value of two hundred thousand.

CECIL: Madam—Sell Crown land?

ELIZABETH: There is a time when thrift becomes extravagant, old man, and this is such a time. The other hundred thousand send to Plymouth. Sir Francis Drake will tell you it will build six ships; tell him it must build me ten. If he must use green timber, so. These ships must float till Parma's great Armada comes; thereafter they may sink for me. You sir—

CECIL going but stops enthralled to see the last of the firework display.

Raise volunteers and send them to the Netherlands to occupy the Duke of Parma there awhile.

DUDLEY: Yes, Your Grace.

ELIZABETH: And muster.

DUDLEY: Yes, Your Grace.

ELIZABETH: And train.

DUDLEY: Yes, Your Grace.

ELIZABETH: And Robin—

DUDLEY: Yes, Your Grace?

ELIZABETH: I am glad to see you.

DUDLEY goes.

CECIL: Madam.

ELIZABETH: What?

CECIL: You are a greater monarch than your father.

She looks at him.

And he was a man among men, Your Grace.

ELIZABETH: Our very thought.

He goes. Perfect stillness for a second. Her face remains rigid but her body crumples; she is exhausted. DAVISON enters.

DAVISON: Your Grace, Señor de Quadra demands instant audience.

ELIZABETH (*revivified*): Nay an he demands it, let him have it.

DAVISON goes; she descends.

DE QUADRA *enters.*

DE QUADRA: How now, Your Grace—!

ELIZABETH: How now, de Quadra, where have you been?

DE QUADRA: Been—? This fortnight I have been outside Your Grace's door—with heavy business for Your Grace.

ELIZABETH: Oh would that I had known; this fortnight I have been so idle that the hours have seemed like fortnights.

DE QUADRA: By Heaven, Your Grace—Your shipbuilders aren't idle!

ELIZABETH (*as accepting a compliment upon her people's industry*): Are they not? Oh good. Nothing so conduces to the welfare of the State as an industrious artisan.

DE QUADRA: My master would know what your shipbuilders do!

ELIZABETH: Well sir, I am not familiar with that business, but I take it they build ships.

DE QUADRA: For what?

ELIZABETH: Why to go a-sailing in.

DE QUADRA: Well certainly Your Grace's talk is idle.
She blinks, but then:

ELIZABETH. Then let us talk of something else.

DE QUADRA: I am to ask Your Grace why there are suddenly a thousand English volunteers who fight against my master in the Netherlands.

ELIZABETH: Fashion, de Quadra, simply fashion. Our young men like to say that they have fought against the Duke of Parma as their silly sisters like to say that they have fetched their ruffs from Paris.

DE QUADRA: I hear Your Grace has sent a hundred thousand crowns to Paris—from your privy purse!

ELIZABETH (*a little pause and then*): For ruffs.

DE QUADRA: Your Grace, if you will make no weightier replies to these my master's just complaints I fear lest the amity between yourself and him may wither, and enmity ensue.

ELIZABETH: Are you instructed to say this?

DE QUADRA: Yes, Your Grace.

ELIZABETH: I'm sorry. (*Calls.*) Walsingham!

WALSINGHAM enters, with dossiers, which he places on the table.

Walsingham, the King of Spain complains that we make ready to defend ourselves against his Great Armada. This gentleman complains that I make light replies. Furnish him with something heavier.

WALSINGHAM: Well sir, this is something heavy.

He dumps into DE QUADRA's arms the topmost of the piled dossiers. DE QUADRA raises his eyebrows.

DE QUADRA: Heavy yes; what else is it?

WALSINGHAM: That sir, is the evidence concerning Father Edward Fenton, who conspired to assassinate Her Majesty and proclaim Mary Stuart in her place—by Spanish force of arms.

DE QUADRA: I know no Father Fenton.

He is about to put back the dossier but WALSINGHAM whips another on top of it.

WALSINGHAM: Nor Thomas Throgmorton?

DE QUADRA: Nor Thomas Throgmorton.

WALSINGHAM: Ha! Nor Roberto Ridolfi, I suppose—? Nor Henry Cockeyn, nor George Douglas, nor George Gifford, Creighton, Paget, Parsons, Holt?

He reels off the list of hated names, dumping dossiers in DE QUADRA's arms, the while DE QUADRA can barely see above them, but he keeps his dignity. Flatly:

DE QUADRA: No.

WALSINGHAM: Now that is strange, for they say they know you.

DE QUADRA: Men under interrogation will say anything.

WALSINGHAM picks up the last dossier which he brought in with him.

WALSINGHAM: Then do you know Anthony Babington?

DE QUADRA: No.

WALSINGHAM: Now that is passing strange. For here are letters to him in your hand.

He adds the dossier to the others.

ELIZABETH: Well sir, is the answer heavy yet?

DE QUADRA: Too heavy, Madam. I am not a sideboard. (*He drops them.*) And His Majesty my master will not have his servants mocked. I'll go, and tell him of this strange proceeding.

ELIZABETH: Do, de Quadra.

> DE QUADRA *going, she arrests him:*

And de Quadra—think us lenient that we let you go.

> DE QUADRA *goes.* ELIZABETH *quietly.*

Ye Gods, Cecil, I think it comes soon.

CECIL: I think so too, Your Grace.

ELIZABETH: What is this Babington?

WALSINGHAM: He is a Catholic Gentleman who plots Your Grace's death on Mary Stuart's behalf.

ELIZABETH: What manner of death has this gentleman provided?

WALSINGHAM: Poison, Madam.

ELIZABETH: Hell and damnation, may I not eat?

> *She thinks. She sags. To* WALSINGHAM.

What can you show?

WALSINGHAM: Why letters, Madam, secret letters, which have passed between them hidden in the backs of books, the soles of shoes—and other guilty tricks!

ELIZABETH: A pox on how they passed—are they proof?

WALSINGHAM: Not proof *pedantic.*

ELIZABETH: Proof is pedantic, Walsingham. And Scotland is her son.

CECIL: The King of Scots. It is a very calculating boy, Your Grace, and relishes his crown. Your Grace might hint . . .

ELIZABETH: Hint what?

CECIL: That if he proved well-governed in the advent of his mother's death—And if Your Grace were not herself to marry and happily deliver of a child—Your Grace might hint that he might look one day, one distant day, to have the Crown of England too.

ELIZABETH: Oh Cecil, you care for me so thoroughly that you have even made ready my winding sheet.

CECIL: Madam—

ELIZABETH: —Do it—Hint—!

Going, pauses to add:

But hearken, Cecil, no more than hint. I may yet prove a freak in Nature. (*To* WALSINGHAM.) And you, my other friend, get proof. Get proof pedantic.

Going again, arrested by:

WALSINGHAM: That is more easy said than done, Your Grace!

ELIZABETH: I do not ask that you should do it easily.

She holds him with her eyes, then goes.

CECIL: Now I think you could get proof.

WALSINGHAM: Instruct me, sir. Mary Stuart is cunning.

CECIL: But mainly she's courageous. And courage is a passion.

WALSINGHAM: So?

CECIL: What luxuries does she enjoy?

WALSINGHAM: The luxuries the Queen allows her. Her state, her visitors, her daily riding in the park.

CECIL: Well then.

WALSINGHAM: No; deprivation would not quench her courage.

CECIL: No, it would inflame it. Passions feed on deprivation. And courage is a flame which, fed enough, will burn the house down in the end. What does she think of her son?

WALSINGHAM: She thinks him loyal and loving.

CECIL: Yes, I think you could get proof.

WALSINGHAM: Davison.

A beat of silence while they wait.

Will you give me authority for this?

CECIL: Oh I think you have it, good Francis. If you are not to do it easily, presumably you are to do it hard.

DAVISON enters.

DAVISON: Sir?

WALSINGHAM: Where's Babington?

DAVISON: Still under interrogation, sir.

WALSINGHAM: Well tell them not to break his fingers.

DAVISON: Very good, sir.

He exits.

CECIL: Why are they not to break his fingers?

WALSINGHAM: Because he is to write.

CECIL: Ah, well sir, I will leave you.

WALSINGHAM: Yes sir, I expect you will.

They go separately. A stable clock chimes, rustic and melancholy. NAU enters, an old man now in sloppy slippers. He is carrying a beer keg which he puts down and anxiously regards, drumming his fingers on it. MARY enters, older too, without head-dress or ruff, keys and scissors hanging from her waist and carrying an embroidery frame. She walks slowly and sits.

MARY: Claud, is it hot or cold today? I cannot tell. Even the weather here prevaricates. What would I not give for one day of honest French weather?

She notes his preoccupation.

What is it, Claud; are you troubled?

NAU: Nay, what should trouble me?

Looks over her shoulder at her work.

Unless the fine embroidered scarf which was to have been mine last Christmas. And I see has made no progress since the Spring.

MARY: The heron had no legs last Spring.

NAU (*peering*): His legs are something insufficient now.

MARY: There was an excellent slave-master lost in you.

A little silence, he glancing again at the keg, she sewing. Then:

MARY: I saw a heron in the Park today. I came so close he hopped into the air all arsy-varsy and asquawking. But then he wafted up, and sailed away, right quietly. No marvel birds do not have souls. If they had souls as well as wings they had been blessed as angels, had they not?

She looks up. Feeling her regard he turns and:

NAU: Madam?

MARY (*putting down her frame*): Nay what a devil *is* it?

NAU: I do not know if I should tell Your Grace.

MARY: Then tell me. And I will tell you if you should have told.

NAU: Look, Your Grace—(*crossing to barrel, plucking out the bung*) —there is a place in here.

MARY: A place?

NAU: A leather pocket, and in it, this.

Takes out a folded letter. She holds out her hand for it.

MARY: Well we have seen the like before; though seldom so ingenious . . .

NAU: Read it, Madam; it's from Babington.

MARY (*more interested*): Oh. (*Reads.*) 'Your Grace, I have acquainted these with the design you know of: Westmorland, Darcy, Cumberland, Arundel, Hamilton—' Hamilton?— good—

NAU: Read on.

MARY: 'They are ready to join it, but only on Your Grace's sure approval. Your Grace's signature to this sets fire to the fuse . . .' (*Slowly.*) My signature to this . . .

NAU: Yes, Your Grace.

MARY: 'Else all fails. Your Grace's humble loving servant, Anthony' . . . Nay, this is something too ingenious . . . Did that come from the castle brewery?

NAU: I do not know.

MARY: Is this his hand?

NAU: I cannot tell.

They peer together at the paper. She murmurs:

MARY: Nor I . . . I have ruined my eyes, on your poxy scarf . . .

A noise off. She folds the paper quickly; he quickly puts the barrel on the floor.

WALSINGHAM enters. He takes an arrogant stand and looks at her. (Stares, astonished.) What—? (*Calls.*) Roget!

WALSINGHAM: I have instructed your people to let us alone.

MARY: And who the devil might you be, sir, to instruct my people?

WALSINGHAM: My name is Walsingham.

MARY *freezes. Then steadily, mildly:*

MARY: Welcome, Sir Francis. You are most timely.

WALSINGHAM: Indeed?

MARY: Yes, for I desire your opinion of this keg of beer.

WALSINGHAM: Of what—?

MARY: This keg of beer, sir. Taste it, for I think it tastes oddly.

WALSINGHAM: Madam, I am not so junior nor have come so far for nothing weightier than to taste your beer—

MARY: —Yet taste it. For I think it tastes of leather.

WALSINGHAM (*frowns, gives it up, shrugs*): Look, lady, don't think to beguile me with some little arbitrary wantonness as if to say that you were nothing worse than childish. I know you what you are. Here, Madam, letters for you.

Thinking over his evident indifference to the keg, she picks up the packet he throws down. She sees the letters blatantly opened and thinks hard again before, cautiously, flatly:

MARY: Walsingham, these letters have been opened.

WALSINGHAM: Henceforth all your letters will be opened. For I have opened those which you have dropped at certain times and certain places, riding in the Park.

MARY: I have dropped no letters, riding in the Park.

WALSINGHAM: You lie.

Her head flies round and NAU *exclaims.*

It is not worth a quarrel. You will ride no more.

MARY *appalled.*

Nor walk outside these rooms.

MARY: . . . Nay let me understand you, sir—

WALSINGHAM: I have a poor opinion of your understanding, Madam, but it should suffice for this—you are to be confined!

NAU: You are not serious?

WALSINGHAM: Who's this?

NAU: I am Her Grace's secretary, sir—

WALSINGHAM: —Then hold your tongue—(*Turning again to* MARY.)

MARY: He is my secretary and my friend!

WALSINGHAM: Still let him hold his tongue. For I have also read the letters which your friends have carried hence when they have visited. In consequence of which henceforward you will have no visitors.

NAU: No visitors—!

WALSINGHAM: And three servants only—

NAU: Three sir—?

WALSINGHAM: Of my choosing. There is another thing—

MARY (*gripping the arms of her chair*): What thing is that?

WALSINGHAM (*pointing to the Cloth of State*): That thing—It comes down.

MARY: . . . Walsingham, come here.

He stands before her.

Do you tell me that I am to be mewed up and deprived of all my retinue?

WALSINGHAM: I do.

MARY: Then you have done your office, get you gone. (*Points to the Cloth of State.*) That stays!

WALSINGHAM: Nay don't attempt the Queen with me—

NAU: —Attempt, sir—Do you dare?

WALSINGHAM (*looking at* MARY): Why what's to dare? Her State's all gone, and God knows in herself I see no Majesty.

Satisfied by her reaction:

Now I'm for London (*Going.*) where I have material matters to attend to.

He goes, briskly. NAU, *tremulous with shock and pity:*

NAU: Oh Madam . . .

She holds up her hand. Her face is white and twisted but not wild.

MARY: Now am I learning self command or losing self-respect? Time was I'd rather have been crucified than sit and suffer censure from a Jack in Office such as that—!

The memory of it gets her to her feet.

An unqualitied, dull cypher such as that! (*Controls herself.*) But no, good Jack, I think this persecution is too gross, too arbitrary—and too hellishly well aimed!

NAU: Madam?

MARY: You know me well. Would you not use me, point by point as he has done, if you desired me to do something desperate?

On the last word she produces the letter. NAU, *horrified:*

NAU: Oh Madam, burn it!

She considers it a second, then tosses it onto the table.

MARY: Aye . . .

She sits.

He'll do as he has said though, Claud.

NAU: Aye; that was hatred.

MARY: 'T'was worse; he is a Puritan, and that was disapproval. He'll save my soul by keeping me walled up. Claud, if I am to be kept walled up I think I shall run mad . . . (*She stares about. Her glance falls on the paper.*) Let's look at that again.

NAU: Nay.

He grabs for it, but she is too quick for him.

MARY: Now I could swear that this is Babington's own hand.

NAU: Oh do not so persuade yourself—That is your death warrant!

MARY: It could be my release. It's not unlikely that these gentlemen should want my name for such an enterprise. It could be my release and *her* death-warrant. By God it were a pity to burn that . . . And what now should I weigh against it?

NAU: Weigh my love against it!

She looks at him and wavers.

Weigh your son against it!

She looks away from him; she sags; she lets the letter fall from her fingers onto the table. Then breathes out a terrible sigh and rests her face upon her hand, eyes covered.

NAU: Oh my poor Mistress . . .

WALSINGHAM *enters. She rouses, growling.*

MARY: We thought that you had gone, sir.

He dumps onto the table the basket that he carries.

Another thing?

He lifts the lid of basket. She goes and face changes, taking from the basket a selection of child's toys. Voice wavering:

These are the presents I have sent to my son.

WALSINGHAM: And your letters.

Takes out and dumps down a wad of letters, taped.

MARY: He—?—He has kept them?

WALSINGHAM: He has never received them.

Tilts basket. She takes out two more billets like the first.

MARY: Never received . . .? Small wonder that he never wrote to *me*!

WALSINGHAM: He has no wish to. Nor to see you. He knows you.

MARY: He—?

WALSINGHAM: He has been instructed, Madam, in the manner of your life; and in the manner of his father's death.

MARY (*whispering, incredulous*): You have blackened me?

WALSINGHAM: How blacken black?

MARY: Nay I think this is some practice, Master Walsingham; you would provoke—(*She fawns on him.*)

WALSINGHAM: —Upon my soul it is the truth!

MARY (*incredulous, pleading*): But of all my letters . . . not one?

WALSINGHAM: Madam, you have had no communication! . . . It is my mistress who has played the mother's part.

He goes. NAU *watches in horror and pity as* MARY, *motionless, slides helplessly into tears which she makes no attempt to hide and then her face darkening and her voice shaking with passion:*

MARY: Oh she . . . She-ee! . . . Shee-ee! . . . *Elizabeth!*

She speeds to the table and snatches up the pen.

NAU: Oh Madam, you will sign away your life!

MARY: Or hers!

NAU: Aye Madam—murder or suicide—think upon your soul!

MARY: Nay God may think on that, it's his! (*Calls.*) Roget!

NAU: Oh what a summing up!

MARY: I have no choice!

NAU: Cowardly, Madam—always we have choice!

MARY: What choice—huh? Six rooms, no sky, and after thirty years maybe lie down and quietly die—And she to have my son? Roget!

BREWER enters. Stands silently.

MARY: Where is my gentleman?

BREWER: Your gentleman's without, Your Grace. He said Your Grace had made complaint about a keg of beer I sent from the brewery.

She points to the keg. He goes, takes out bung, looks in, finds nothing, looks at her, all very deliberate.

MARY: Who are you, sir?

BREWER: I am an English Catholic and Your Grace's subject. I am to take a matter from Your Grace to Father Flint in Chesterfield.

MARY: And he to take it where?

BREWER: We are a chain of trust, Your Grace. Each knows his neighbour and no more.

MARY: Take it then.

He comes and takes the letter she holds out, but as he is going back:

But if you take it to Elizabeth—

He spins, indignant:

BREWER: —Nay now you wrong me!

MARY: Be reasonable, sir, it may be so. And if it is, we only ask that you should tell our sister that before we die we'd have one day—nay one half day, of conversation with our son. Ask this of her charity.

BREWER (*angry*): Nay an' you suppose I take this to Elizabeth I will not take it anywhere.

MARY (*licks her lips, then*): Sir, I have made my choice. (*Going.*) And you—whatever choice it is that you have made—(*half order, half desperate appeal*)—make haste!

She goes, NAU *following. Enter* WALSINGHAM, CECIL. WALSINGHAM *goes to* BREWER *and takes the letter. Turns as* ELIZABETH *enters slowly dressed in fantastic black. He plonks the letter on the table before her:*

WALSINGHAM: Proof, Your Grace.

ELIZABETH looks down at it. CECIL *puts a document before her.*

CECIL: The warrant, for her execution.

ELIZABETH glances unwillingly at it. Then to BREWER:

ELIZABETH: Did she say anything?

BREWER: She said I was to ask Your Grace if—

ELIZABETH: What? She knew that you would bring this *here*?

BREWER: She did suspect it, Madam; and she said I was to ask—

ELIZABETH: —Nay . . . Then do not tell me what she asked.

She dips the pen. She licks her lips and looks round for a reprieve. To CECIL:

Is there nothing from Scotland?

CECIL: This, Your Grace. It is the most discreet, far-sighted child I ever met.

She takes the letter which he gives her and waves them all off. Alone, she looks at the letter. Looks up from it and:

ELIZABETH: Oh; little boy . . .

She puts down the letter, takes up the pen and signs, calling:

Davison!

DAVISON *enters, in black.*

Do you see that?

DAVISON *looks at the signed warrant.*

DAVISON: I see it, Your Grace.

ELIZABETH: What will you do with it?

DAVISON: I will take it to Sheffield, Your Grace.

ELIZABETH: You will do it without authority and I shall put you in the Tower for it.

DAVISON: May I know for how long, Your Grace?

ELIZABETH: Until such time as the world recognizes that it was not my desire.

DAVISON: I do not think the world will be deceived by this, Your Grace. (*A flick of resentment.*) Nor by Your Grace's mourning.

She looks at him fathomless, then:

ELIZABETH: The world is deceived by nothing. The world must be given something by which to seem to be deceived ... Well sir, do it.

She mounts towards the throne. DAVISON *picks up warrant, and then:*

DAVISON: I think you burden me too much, Your Grace. Your Grace must tell me what to do.

ELIZABETH: Why, man—your office!

Drums, cloth of state eclipsed by black cloth of mourning. Two black clad SERVANTS *unroll a black carpet. Enter* MARY, ATTENDANTS, NAU, PRIEST, *all in black.* MARY *stands at the head of the carpet and looks along it, head high but held sideways as though unable to look directly at what is at the end of it, off stage.*

MARY: So there they are, the axe and block. How practical they look. (*To* NAU.) Love, you have stayed with me long. Spare yourself this last?

NAU: An' it please Your Grace, I'll stay a little longer yet.

MARY: Here then; a memento of my idleness; your still un-finished scarf.

Taking it, he breaks down.

Hush now!

DAVISON: Are you ready, Madam?

MARY (*formal*): I claim God's fatherly protection for my son; and Christ's incomprehensible compassion for my soul.

ALL: Amen.

MARY: I'm ready now, sir.

She moves but DAVISON *kneels quickly before her.*

DAVISON: Pardon.

MARY: For what?

DAVISON: Your Grace, I brought the warrant.

He looks up at her. She frowns.

MARY: Is it not Davison?

DAVISON: Your Grace.

She touches his hair absently.

MARY: Be comfortable, William. The thing you brought was nothing much. A death-warrant requires a royal signature. And I signed my own.

She moves, looks off again at the axe and block, isolated.

And if your Great and Virgin Queen should wonder why I signed it, you are to tell her this: There is more living in a death that is embraced than in a life that is avoided across three score years and ten. And I embrace it—thus!

She throws off the black, revealing scarlet head to foot.

Davison.

DAVISON: Madam?

MARY: Now.

Plunges off along the carpet. They tumble after, taken by surprise. Drum beat. Stops convulsively. CECIL *enters. Looks at* ELIZABETH, *cautiously.*

ELIZABETH: She was an adulterous, disorderly, lecherous strumpet!

CECIL: Yes, Your Grace.

ELIZABETH: She was a *fool*!

CECIL: Yes, Your Grace.

ELIZABETH: She was—Nay there are no words for saying she was. Only words for saying what she was not.

CECIL approaches the foot of the throne. Seriously, persuasively:

CECIL: As: worthy; thoughtful; self-denying; diligent; prepared.

She looks at him attentive, mistrustful.

Your Grace, next year or the next, Spain sends against us his Invincible Armada. And we shall astonish them! And as their great ships founder and they drown they will cry out: 'How? How is this possible?' And our cannon will tell them: 'Elizabeth! Elizabeth made it possible!' And they will hear it across Europe in Madrid—!—Aye Madam, they will hear it across Europe—and down Centuries.

In the ringing silence left by his rhetoric her voice comes hard and dead.

ELIZABETH: Very like, Master Cecil; very like . . .

She almost snarls:

And then?

She rises painfully, and makes towards Exit. A triumphant fanfare. She ignores it.

THE CURTAIN FALLS

COMMENTARY

COMMENTARY BY E. R. WOOD

A Modern Problem in a Historical Setting

After reading the author's Introduction you will be aware of the difference between dramatised History and drama in a historical setting. The pure historian is concerned with accurate information about the past. Detail matters to him; evidence is essential. Where one piece of evidence is inconsistent with another, he must consider both; when he does not know, he is under an obligation to say so. This would not suit a theatre audience. The playwright is expected to present the broad sweep of events; he is interested in motives and consequences. He cannot do with 'perhaps' and 'on the other hand' and 'the evidence is inconclusive'. He has to select and telescope his material so as to make an immediate impact on an audience. He sees it shaping into a pattern from which a positive view of human life emerges.

Robert Bolt likes to set his plays in historical times, but he is always writing about today. *Vivat! Vivat Regina!* is about 'the penalties of Power,' he says, 'the sacrifice of self which Power demands, and gets, and squanders—to what purpose?' This is poignantly illustrated in the interwoven lives of Elizabeth I and Mary Queen of Scots. We have a double interest in such historical characters: the strangeness and remoteness of their lives as compared with ours, and the relevance of their experience for our own time. The troubles and triumphs of two Sixteenth Century queens need no longer rouse our indignation or disturb our sleep, so we can enjoy them: yet one of their common problems remains; high office still demands sacrifices of the personal life. It is appropriate that the play deals with two women, for in the modern power world, too, it is among young women that the mutilation can be most marked, because of their biological and emotional make-up.

Such a subject could be examined on an intellectual level by a historian or a sociologist. It is the special art of the playwright to bring it home to us through the imagination and intuition. He can bring his queens to life, aided by the art and understanding of his players and director, so as to make us feel what it was like to be Mary Stuart or Elizabeth Tudor. This is something quite different from ascertaining and relating the ascertainable facts of their lives, as the historian does.

The Dramatist's way with History

The author of *Vivat! Vivat Regina!* has selected, from all that those two remarkable women did and said and suffered, only what is relevant to his theme, and only as much as can be effectively presented in a theatre in one evening. He has had to practise severe self-denial, for in the story of either there is much that it would be tempting to bring in—exciting, inspiring, appalling, touching, amusing—that has to be left out because it might blur the clear lines of the play or spin it out too long. Characters like John Knox or Bothwell might easily take over the play, or romantic episodes like Mary's escape from Loch Leven might lure the playwright away from his purpose.

He has to be always conscious of how much—or how little—an audience can be expected to take in. Think, for instance, of the multiplicity of important persons associated with Elizabeth and Mary over a space of twenty years, and the problem of choosing from them the individuals who can be made interesting to, and easily recognisable by, a theatre audience. In the Scotland of Mary Stuart duplicity was so common a feature of her nobles that it is difficult to follow their intentions. Such people are a nuisance on the stage, where we need to know which side characters are on. One of Mary's most important counsellors was her illegitimate half-brother the Earl of Moray. On her return from France, he gave her political advice and support, and even something resembling brotherly affection; but when she married Darnley he rebelled and mustered troops to fight her. She distinguished herself by leading an army against him, and driving him to take refuge in England. He returned for a further period of favour and influence, and supported her rather equivocally in the crisis after the murder of Rizzio. But when she was imprisoned at Loch Leven he forced her to sign an instrument of abdication, and proclaimed himself Regent. He shared with Morton command of the army that defeated her at Langside, and after her flight to England he supplanted her and became her most malignant enemy. When he was assassinated in an Edinburgh street in 1570, a grateful Mary granted a pension to his assassin. Now this fascinating Scotsman does not appear in *Vivat! Vivat Regina!* No doubt a fine play could be written about the relations between the royal brother and sister but for *Vivat! Vivat Regina!* (which is about Mary and Elizabeth) we want a single Scottish leader as spokesman for the opposition to Mary—someone clear-cut, consistent, always recognisable. So the author makes a convincing stage character of Morton—the essence of what Mary had to contend with—cynical, ruthless, drily ironical. Morton in fact was pretty devious too, but in relation to Mary it was clear where he stood, and it is clear in the play. Morton takes over some of Moray's historical role and the audience is spared the confusions and complications of historical truth.

Another stage character who conveniently takes on the similar roles of other historical characters is Nau. The playwright needs a loyal retainer who can attend on Mary from her girlhood in France, through her triumphs and troubles in Scotland to her nineteen years' imprisonment in England, and be with her at her tragic end. No single person did that. The real Claud Nau did some of it, but he did not enter her service till 1575 (his brother had served her earlier) and he was not with her at the end because he had betrayed her to Walsingham, so that his evidence had been used against her at her trial. She had thought she could trust him; she had always confided in him. He himself probably thought he would be faithful and loyal to the end, until the threat of torture put him to the test. But the play is not about Nau, nor about loyalty and treachery in the service of Mary. A scrupulous adherence to the historical facts might have pulled the play out of shape,

turning our minds away from Mary's courage and consideration
for others in her last hours, to bitter reflections on a secondary
character. Nau serves the audience well as a consistent, affectionate,
wise and trusted counsellor, the one steady and reliable man whom
Mary can turn to through all her turmoils.

Just as Mary in her time had many secretaries, here represented
by the one stage character of Nau, so at Elizabeth's court there was
a series of Spanish ambassadors, all merged here in the one
recognisable figure of de Quadra. There is a splendid scene in the
play where Walsingham overwhelms the Spanish ambassador
with a pile of heavy dossiers about the many plots, fomented by
Spain over a long period of years, against the Queen's life.
De Quadra had been dead twenty-five years when the last of
these plots was exposed. It may be important to the historian that
the ambassador by now was Mendoza, but not to the playwright,
who is devising a dramatic way of showing that Walsingham has
accumulated a vast quantity of evidence of Spanish implication
in conspiracies, and that a time came when Elizabeth was ready for
a show-down. Having already built up a character to represent
the Spanish role in Elizabeth's affairs, he cannot afford to let him
die of the Plague in 1662 in the interests of historical accuracy.
We in the audience don't want to get to know his successors:
we enjoy seeing this man confounded, the same Spaniard we have
watched dabbling in English affairs from the first. There is no
falsification of History in this, only gross simplification. Nobody
is actually misled.

The scene of the dossiers is only one of many confrontations
and encounters expressing in stage terms historical situations and
developments which were less clear-cut in reality. The playwright
often telescopes distance and time in order to present the essence
of a situation. His concentration on the essential elements by
boldly cutting out detail is something like the work of a gifted
artist who shows all we need to see in a few strokes of pencil or
brush. Robert Bolt's treatment of History comes from a happy

blending of gifts, skills and experience: first, the orthodox training of a historian (he read History at Manchester University before he began to write); then the flair for cutting through masses of detail to what really matters, developed by practice (such as the preparation of the film script of *Doctor Zhivago*, for which he had to condense the novel to one-twentieth of its length); and then the dramatist's firm grasp of what is effective on the stage.

Stage Presentation

The last-named skill involves the problems (familiar to Shakespeare and his contemporaries) of how to cram within the confined space and time of a theatrical presentation the events of half a lifetime and the scope of three kingdoms. Robert Bolt has triumphed by exploiting the full resources of a modern theatre and by encouraging players and audience to think of the stage as a fluid acting area capable of representing different places in rapid succession, or even simultaneously. By the enterprising use of fly tower and lighting, Hampton Court can become Holyrood in a few seconds. But once we have broken free of time and space, the stage needs not necessarily represent either palace: a dance in Edinburgh, interrupted by a loud explosion in an off-stage area which the audience readily accepts as the scene of Darnley's murder, darkens into a dream-like movement of vague figures; as the lights come up we realise that we are looking at the power-struggle in Europe, including England, Spain and the Vatican, while Mary sits on a throne above with Darnley's murderer and supplanter at her side. All Europe is watching her and reacting to her guilt or involvement.

This kind of staging is not merely convenient and practical as a means of presenting world events: it is theatrically and imaginatively exciting in itself. *Vivat! Vivat Regina!* was first produced at Chichester, where the theatre has features that recall the Elizabethan stage, but modern equipment that gives it greater flexibility than Shakespeare dreamt of.

Language

Just as Robert Bolt cuts away the details to compress sixteen years of plotting into a few minutes of stage action, so he pares down language to essentials. For example, when Elizabeth, unwilling to appoint Leicester to an army command, suggests alternatives, not a word is wasted:

> ELIZABETH: Suffolk?
>
> CECIL: Too old, Your Grace.
>
> ELIZABETH: Mountjoy?
>
> CECIL: Too young.
>
> ELIZABETH: Recall the Earl—of Leicester.

(There is a double economy here, for the actress playing Elizabeth, by singing out the last line formally, not to Cecil but to the air, makes it the cue for a change of scene, time, mood, and for Leicester's entrance.)

She is at once busy with crisp questions and instructions, ending with a message of relenting affection that is all the more eloquent for being matter-of-fact in style:

> ELIZABETH: You, sir—Raise volunteers and send them to the Netherlands to occupy the Duke of Parma there awhile.
>
> DUDLEY: Yes, Your Grace.
>
> ELIZABETH: And muster.
>
> DUDLEY: Yes, Your Grace.
>
> ELIZABETH: And train.
>
> DUDLEY: Yes, Your Grace.
>
> ELIZABETH: And Robin—
>
> DUDLEY: Yes, Your Grace?
>
> ELIZABETH: I am glad to see you.

In her Council nobody is allowed circumlocutions or verbiage:

> CECIL: It is quite certain that the King of Spain will marry his son to Mary Stuart.
>
> ELIZABETH: Well then, it is certain.
>
> CECIL: Your Grace, it must not be.
>
> ELIZABETH: What then? (*Cecil does not answer*)

WALSINGHAM: It cannot be, Your Grace; war rather.

CECIL: War with Spain . . . ?

ELIZABETH: What then? Speak!

CECIL: Spain would not marry Scotland, if he could marry
here.

The brevity is the very reverse of poverty of matter or vocabulary. It suits the character of Elizabeth as presented in this play—
dry, pithy, sardonic. Robert Bolt has resisted the temptation to
enrich the play with some of the resounding eloquence attributed
to Gloriana in historical records: when he uses her actual sayings
they are the cases where brevity is the soul of wit—and an astrin-
gent wit at that. The lines he has invented for her have the same
ring. When told that the people will not accept Alencon as a
husband for her, she answers: 'Nor will we; so send 100,000
crowns to him, to keep his relish for our person keen.'

But laconic speech is not confined to the court of Elizabeth.
Mary too comes sharply to the heart of any matter, and so do her
court. If Elizabeth has the best lines in the play, it is because they
express a character and a situation where her dry wit is appropriate.

The quality of the language comes not only from condensa-
tion: the author has an advantage in having set his play in an age
when English speech was virile in vocabulary, vivid in imagery
and harmonious in its cadences. The savour of Elizabethan idiom
is here achieved without phoney archaism by a blending of
authentic sayings from History with new-minted or adapted
ones, all set in a general flow of dialogue which sounds modern
but without being tied to any particular time or place. All of it
seems to have the old virtues, none of the jaded cliché of today.
No modern civil servant could report: 'There is such hammering
in the Spanish shipyards that Spain shakes.' No head of state today
would refer to an opponent as 'this slippery villain'; what we have
gained in the graces of political life we have lost in vigour and
directness of speech.

An extra boon for the author is the irruption into his play of
craggy Scots such as John Knox, Morton and Bothwell, with the

rugged force of their native accent and dialect, so well tuned to their grim humour and mood.

In the last minute of the play the contrasted styles of speech express contrasted views of life and history. Cecil's rhetoric suits the heroic theme of Elizabeth's role in England's glory. It is not empty or false: Elizabeth's fame *was* heard across Europe and down the Centuries. But the Queen, instead of responding with stirring eloquence from the heart and stomach of a mighty prince, brings us back with her bitter irony to the realities behind the royal greatness; we leave the theatre pondering the bleak scepticism of her last two words—'And then?'.

E. R. WOOD

NOTES

NOTES BY E. R. WOOD

The notes that follow are intended to provide a running commentary on the text for the benefit of the reader interested in the historical basis of the play. Some of them expand or elucidate historical references: others point out the rearrangement or pruning or distillation of historical detail which the playwright has found necessary or advantageous. If the reader concludes that it is risky to treat the play as a piece of History accurate in every detail, he or she will be right. This is not to say that in its essence it is any less true. There is nothing positively false—only the understood and acceptable falsity of enormous simplification and compression. The History is arranged to present a kind of thematic truth, and the reader is invited to assess the skill and impressive force with which the essentials of a situation are highlighted.

Robert Bolt read the draft of these notes, and his comments have been incorporated where appropriate.

Page 1. *Mary in France.* When the play opens Mary is 17 years old. She had
succeeded to the throne of Scotland at the age of six days, when her
father, James V, died of misery after the rout of his army by the
English at Solway Moss; and she was formally crowned Queen of
Scotland at the age of nine months. When she was five she was sent
to France, while her mother, Mary of Guise, remained in Scotland
engaged in a struggle for power. (She became Regent in 1554,
after which she ruled Scotland, with French troops to sustain her
against the rebellious Scots protestants, until her death of dropsy
in 1560.)

In France, Mary was brought up partly by her powerful and
ambitious Guise relations and partly at the court of Henry II, who
always intended that she should marry his son Francis. According
to her recent biographer, Antonia Fraser (*Mary Queen of Scots*,
Weidenfeld and Nicolson 1969 and Panther books, 1970), she
had a happy childhood there: 'In marked contrast to her cousin,
Elizabeth Tudor, she enjoyed an exceptionally cosseted youth. . . .
She was tended by a cocoon of servants and other satellites, whose
only duty was to nurture the royal nurselings in as great luxury
as possible.' She was evidently a charming and accomplished
child, much admired at court. But the first scene here emphasises
that she lacked a mother, because her mother was too busy with
the affairs of a far-off country to give her love. When she was
married in April 1558, her mother was not at the very splendid
wedding. Mary was a beautiful (so everybody said) girl of 16; the
Dauphin a sickly, backward, unprepossessing boy a year her
junior—but he was the heir to the throne of France. Only 15
months later Henry II was killed in an accident at his favourite
sport of jousting, and Mary was Queen of France. From now on,
whether she liked it or not she was involved in politics.

Nau. He was a Guise retainer who really came into Mary's service
much later. He is here used as a convenient means of presenting
to the audience some essential facts of Mary's upbringing and
present situation.

A kind of love. Whether Mary of Guise loved her daughter or not,
she was keenly interested in her, keeping in touch by regular
correspondence. When she visited France for some months in
1550, she delighted in the company of her little girl. When Mary

of Guise died in June 1560, the young Mary was seriously ill with grief at the news, though she had not seen her mother for nine years. This grief is apparent at the end of this scene. It is not inconsistent with her bitterness towards a mother who had let herself be separated from her child by affairs of state.

Page 2. *my child*. A touch of dramatic irony here. Mary little knew that she was to have a child from whom she would be separated for ever when he was ten months old. There is further irony in the fact that it was indeed to be 'no care of state' that would lead her to abandon her child—but rather her perverse passion for Bothwell.

Understands her misconception. She thinks he was party to the political marriage to Francis.

Page 3. *your English Kingdom*. Mary had a strong claim to the throne of England. When Mary Tudor died in November, 1558, Henry II of France had his daughter-in-law proclaimed Queen of England, and the Dauphin and Mary jointly assumed the royal arms of England, an action which Elizabeth was to hold against Mary for the rest of her life. To the Catholic world, Mary's claim was better than Elizabeth's. They did not accept the annulment of Henry VIII's first marriage (refused by the Pope), so they could not recognise his marriage to Anne Boleyn; consequently they regarded Anne's daughter Elizabeth as illegitimate. Mary Stuart was a legitimate great-granddaughter of Henry VII, whose daughter Margaret had married James IV of Scotland. Their son James V was Mary's father. On the other hand, Henry VIII's will had debarred foreigners from the succession, and Mary, being half Scots and half French, was certainly a foreigner.

Mary of Guise made the match to make sure of a Scottish-French alliance, which would permanently commit French troops to the defence of Scotland (against English intervention). She may also have had her eye on the English succession, though at that time it was not in doubt, the English throne being occupied by a young and indisputably legitimate Tudor—Edward VI.

Page 4. *I pray for him to die*. If she did, her prayers were soon answered. The poor lad died in December 1560. Mary is said to have abandoned herself to passionate grief. She was also rumoured to have poisoned him, but accusations of poisoning were common in those days when any important person died. The Queen Mother, Catherine de Medici, was also thought to have poisoned him. Politically, Mary had everything to lose by his death.

You have high office. Nau is making the point, which Mary accepts and at the same time resents, that royalty is a high vocation which demands sacrifice of personal happiness.

The treaty which your mother has negotiated. The Treaty of Edinburgh was actually signed after Mary of Guise's death. In it the French agreed not to press Mary's claim to the English throne; but Mary never ratified the treaty.

Page 5. *The English army.* Elizabeth had sent ships and soldiers to the Scots Protestants to help them to drive out the French forces, there to uphold Mary of Guise. The Treaty of Edinburgh provided that both English and French forces should be withdrawn, and the government of Scotland should pass to a council of Scots nobles.

The more the Queen the more I am myself. The crucial argument here is that the queen does not have to sacrifice herself as a person. The conclusion to be drawn from the play is that she must. Mary failed as a queen because she indulged herself as a woman: Elizabeth had to deny herself as a woman in order to become a great queen. At this stage it seems that it is Elizabeth who is about to ruin her prospects as a queen by marrying to please herself; Mary seems wise and ready to take advice, while Elizabeth is wilful and rash.

Page 6. *Robert Dudley.* He was a nobleman, but his origins were not auspicious; both his father, the Duke of Northumberland, who plotted to make Lady Jane Grey queen on the death of Edward VI, and his grandfather, had been executed for treason. He was a tall, handsome, accomplished courtier, very attractive to the young queen Elizabeth. He had been married for ten years. A sinister feature of the death of his wife, Amy Robsart, was the persistent report *beforehand* that Dudley intended to get rid of her. (But see note on Page 109.) Nau is represented here as having foreknowledge of what was to happen. Such forecasts were whispered around Europe.

Your royal mother charged me thus. The message from Mary of Guise once more harps on the theme that affairs of state matter more than private feelings. Mary is filled with surprise and admiration to learn of her mother's dedication. This is typical of what the author calls her 'leonine largeness of spirit: a great queen if she hadn't insisted on being a great woman first.' Throughout this interview she wavers between two opposite sides in this conflict of attitudes.

Page 7. *Change of Scene.* The change from France to England is briskly managed. Whatever decoration of leaves and flowers was provided to suggest a French exterior is now drawn up into the flies (the space above the stage), from which an English court setting descends. If the stage offers no such facilities, something simple and swift, such as attendants bearing emblems or banners, accompanied by lighting-change, can be devised instead. The opening words, heralding the entry of Elizabeth, echo the closing words of the previous scene, marking the exit of Mary. This is an openly theatrical artifice; it is also meaningful, in line with the seesaw of attention on the two queens.

Elizabeth. She was 25 at this time, already autocratic, and more assured than her uncertain situation seemed to warrant. She grows in political stature throughout the play.

Cecil. He was a man of 38, a middle-class, Cambridge-educated civil servant, ruled by intellect, not emotion. J. E. Neale says in his life of Elizabeth: 'His capacity for work, his care for detail, his grasp of difficulties, amounted to genius; and if ever there was a perfect minister, it was he. No step was more propitious at the opening of Elizabeth's reign than his appointment as Principal Secretary.' In this play he stands throughout for the proposition that private life must be sacrificed to the good of the state. Elizabeth's relationship with Cecil, though stormy, was one of trust.

This scene concentrates in sharply defined dramatic form the clash of personalities and attitudes spread over several months and many people. Even before the death of Amy Robsart, the scandal connecting Dudley and the Queen, resounding through Europe, had driven Cecil to talk of resigning. He actually told de Quadra (by no means a close friend) that Dudley was thinking of killing his wife. The next day Amy Robsart was found dead, with a broken neck, at the foot of the stairs in her country house near Oxford. Robert Dudley's explanation given in the play, unconvincing though it sounds, was probably the truth. A coroner's jury returned a verdict of accidental death, but there is strong evidence for suicide. Elizabeth was convinced of Dudley's innocence, and fluctuated for nearly a year between defiance of critics or gossip, and caution. During this time Cecil was in and out of favour, in inverse proportion to Dudley's popularity at Court. Finally Elizabeth's brain triumphed over her heart, or her concern for the country triumphed over her personal wishes, and the crisis passed, though the affair with Dudley lingered on for some years, giving periodical anxiety to Cecil.

Page 11.. *If the Queen takes you to bed*. This is a slightly improved version of a prophecy attributed to de Quadra.

My father killed my mother and disowned me. Henry VIII cast off Queen Catherine in order to marry Anne Boleyn in the hope of a male heir. On September 7th, 1533 Anne disappointed everybody by giving birth to a girl—Elizabeth. When her next baby was born dead, Anne was accused of adultery (with several men) and on May 19th, 1536, she was executed. She was probably innocent. An excuse was found to annul the marriage, so that the child Elizabeth was declared illegitimate. Her complaint of deprivation of parental love is parallel to Mary's in the first scene. They both exaggerate their misery. Henry VIII was quite proud of the child Elizabeth because she was quick-witted and a success as a scholar under some famous tutors. She enjoyed the affection of her half-brother Edward and her stepmother, Queen Catherine Parr. She certainly had to learn caution after her father's death, under the Protector Somerset and her half-sister Mary Tudor.

Page 12. *Thunder. Enter Knox*. The thunder and rain are partly symbolical of the reception awaiting the young queen on her home-coming, especially at the hands of John Knox and his followers. In fact her return did coincide with several days of bad weather, exceptional even for Scotland. Knox interpreted it as a black omen for the country; for the queen the effect must have been particularly dispiriting.

The ironic opening of the scene is a grim joke addressed direct to the modern audience (compare the relationship to his audience of the Common Man in *A Man for All Seasons*). Knox goes on to sum up the Calvinist revolution that had recently transformed Scotland, in the forceful language typical of his sermons and polemical writings.

Knox ('The Moses of Scotland') throve on conflict and recorded in his autobiographical writings how he trounced the great in arguments; so he is a ready-made theatrical character, coming to us with dramatic confrontations already realised and some of the dialogue already provided. He had first been ordained as a Catholic priest, but had broken away to preach the reformed (originally Lutheran) religion. Scotland had long been in the middle of a tug-of-war between mainly Protestant England and mainly Catholic France. During a time of French domination (while Mary of Guise was in power) Knox had served a prison sentence on French galleys, an experience that had embittered his hatred of the Catholics. Later he had thriven as a preacher and theologist in England, but had had to flee to the Continent when Mary Tudor succeeded Edward VI. In Geneva he learnt from Calvin how a church could be a democracy of laymen choosing their own ministers. He also absorbed a grim and joyless theology. When he returned to Scotland in 1559 he found it overripe for the popular reform movement, because the wealth and power of the old Church were widely hated in a country so poor. He also found support in the middle and upper classes.

The author points out that by an amazing piece of 'drama by history', Knox was a galley slave in the French fleet sent to bring the infant Mary from Scotland. His family overlords were the Bothwells.

When Mary Stuart arrived in 1561 the Scottish Parliament had just abolished the authority of the Pope and prohibited the Mass on pain of death. To Knox it must have seemed that a Catholic queen was a threat to everything they had gained. In fact she was in favour of toleration.

drape. An embroidered cloth depicting Virgin and Child. This stands for Rome, while the simple cross stands for Geneva. Here (and later in the scene with the Anglican bishop) the business with drapes provides a comic element.

yon fat lad. He takes vindicative pleasure in one of the few atrocities staining the Scottish reformation. In 1546 George Wishart, the reformer who had converted Knox, had been strangled and burnt at St. Andrews while Cardinal Beaton and other bishops looked on.

Later the Cardinal was murdered by a Protestant mob, who hung his mutilated body naked from the castle wall. Knox took no part in this incident, but he approved.

Page 13. *First Blast of the Trumpet.* This attack on the rule (regiment) of women (originally published in Geneva in 1558 and intended to be the first of a series) referred to Queen Mary Tudor, but the assertion that 'it is more than a monster in Nature that a woman should reign and bear empire over men' could be applied to Mary of Guise and later Mary Queen of Scots and Queen Elizabeth. Elizabeth was furious, and Knox ruefully said: 'My first blast hath blown from me all my friends in England.' He tried to make his peace with Elizabeth, without actually withdrawing a word, but she was not appeased. Cecil reported that the name of Knox was 'of all others the most odious at Court.'

a wee trumpet in the hands of the Almighty. Not a joke; he meant it.

the mysterious death of her wee French husband. Knox was by no means alone in suggesting that she had killed her husband, or that she was wanton. He had a malicious tongue, all the more powerful because he claimed to be speaking for the Almighty.

Light change. This scene is a good example of the author's gift for distilling the essence of a historical situation in stage presentation and a page of dialogue. The bagpipe is contrasted with the lute, the bright silks of the party from France with the sombre plaids of the Scots, the graceful grouping of one party with the stiff line of the other. The bagpipe suggests the wild barbarism of Scotland, the lute suggests the refinement and dalliance of the French court. Mary's love of colour, of music, song and dance was regarded with dour disapproval by the puritanical Scots.

Certain characters who are to be important later are established in the mind of the audience from the outset. Rizzio, on this our first sight of him, is already provoking the jealousy and hostility of the Lords who will later murder him. (Does it matter that in fact he did not arrive with Mary? He came a year or so later, among the attendants on the Ambassador of Savoy, and he was soon employed by Mary as a musician. Later he became her Latin secretary. Ultimately he rose to favour and influence until his arrogance united hostile groups against him. In the theatre we cannot keep him waiting in the wings until his historical cue calls.)

Bothwell, as Lord High Admiral, had indeed been responsible for bringing Mary from France by sea. (She had asked Elizabeth for safe conduct through England, but this had been refused until she would ratify the Treaty of Edinburgh.) This tough Border chieftain, who is later to sweep her off her feet and ruin her life, already interests the young queen. She thanks him graciously, then, remembering his reputation as a sheep rustler, tries to admonish him, speaking as queen to subject, but is rebuffed with a cheeky compliment as from a familiar young man to a desirable wench. Her reaction, as so often later, is a mixture: she is openly offended at his familiarity and secretly attracted by his bold masculinity.

Her passage with Morton is more uncomfortable; for he upsets her easy assumption that the lords will accept her royal authority. He makes it clear that without troops at her command she is a powerless girl. She was to be well aware of this in her later career. At the head of a loyal army she was a courageous and triumphant queen; but when her troops deserted her she was a humiliated weeping woman.

So this scene gives glimpses of what is to come. These harsh realities did not become as clear as this immediately on her arrival. Public rejoicings in her first few days probably fostered her illusions. But not for long; her first Sunday was marred by an ugly brawl as she went to Mass, and the following Sunday Knox preached a fierce sermon against her.

Page 14. *Our cousin Elizabeth.* Mary and Elizabeth made serious efforts to be friends. Several times they planned 'summit meetings', at which they hoped to settle differences; but their intentions were frustrated by unforeseen obstacles and mutual mistrust. They never met.

Harry Percy. Harry Percy, Earl of Northumberland, was a feudal autocrat and a prominent Catholic. As such, he was not a particularly loyal subject of Queen Elizabeth. He and Bothwell, as Border Lords, were virtually independent of their sovereigns; they had private wars.

When Mary tries to assert her royal authority, Bothwell is unabashed. Morton then shows even less deference. The shock reaches its climax with the insolence of Knox.

Page 15. *Revelation.* Knox was always able to cite Scripture for his purpose, and the Book of Revelation has the advantage that people can make its obscure prophecies mean what they like. (People today find references in it to Nuclear warfare!) The passage in question is in Chapter 17.

The disputation which follows is typical of Knox's style. Mary thought she could beat him in argument or win him over by reason, and on several occasions she sent for him to discuss his latest onslaught on her and her faith. He often reduced her to tears and she once wept so copiously that (as Knox reported with grim humour) her chamber-boy could scarcely get napkins enough to dry up the tears, 'and the owling, besides womanly weeping, stayed her speech.'

Page 16. *avanti*. Go on!

    the Mass. The argument about the Mass sums up very briefly the theological seed of the Reformation and the moral conflict (the individual soul versus the Church) arising from it or expressed by it.

Page 18. *Make a marriage*. He wanted her to marry a Protestant, such as the Scots Earl of Arran or the English Earl of Leicester, and such a marriage was thought a possibility. Mary certainly carried out her threat—far more unfortunately than she could have foreseen—of making a marriage disastrous for the country. Knox also felt it impossible for a woman ruler to survive. (Elizabeth did, but only by turning herself into a man—as she reflects in the play.)

    God save the Queen. We have seen the austere, sin-obsessed challenge of Calvinism to the old Catholic faith, corrupted by power and wealth. Now we have an amusing contrast—the bland compromising Church of England. Unlike Calvinism, which was democratic, the English Reformation was established by the monarchy to suit its purposes (the matrimonial needs of Henry VIII) and supported by an upper class that gained from the plunder of the old Church. It has remained a pillar of the Establishment, so that the satirical tone of the opening of this scene amuses a modern audience in a way that Elizabethans would not have understood. The Bishop is able to step half out of his period and gently reprove the theatre audience for their laughter.

    Scylla and Charybdis. Opposite extremes of danger (originally threatening Ulysses).

Page 19. *the block and the bonfire*. After the hundreds of burnings in the previous reign, the age of Elizabeth was fairly moderate in religious persecution. Catholics were hideously tortured and executed (as we see later in the play) but not for being Catholics—unless they plotted against the Queen.

Page 20. The exchanges of letters—a demonstration of the advantages of flexible staging so freely developed in this play—serve to show Elizabeth adapting her religious preferences to suit the conveniences of power politics. She changes her mind if it is expedient. Later, she will even appoint a 'rampant Papist' to placate Spain, so as to prolong negotiations for a possible, though unlikely, marriage. She rejects the advice of her ministers, Cecil, a moderate but steady Protestant, and Walsingham, a more fanatical one (see page 26). *Geneva:* the source of Calvinism.

Dunelmiensis. Of Durham.

Page 21. *King of Spain.* Mary and Elizabeth both needed to marry if only to produce heirs. They inevitably became rivals for any eligible princes in Europe. It was vital for Elizabeth that Mary should be prevented from marrying Don Carlos, son of Philip II of Spain. Although he was a sickly, ill-tempered, gluttonous epileptic, he would bring to a marriage the power of Catholic Spain, so threatening Elizabeth, Protestant England and the Reformation everywhere. So Elizabeth opened negotiations with a view to marrying Don Carlos herself. (The difference of religion was not an insuperable obstacle). Then she offered to let Mary marry Robert Dudley, and created him Earl of Leicester to improve his qualification. The thought of passing on her lover to her cousin may have been painful, but politically it was an excellent idea. The Queen of Scotland, married to an Englishman whom Elizabeth could trust, would cease to be a danger to England. The two countries might be friends! If Mary wanted a glamorous husband, Leicester was a big improvement on Don Carlos. But Mary was not grateful: descended as she was from Charlemagne and Robert the Bruce, she regarded Elizabeth as a parvenu and called Dudley 'The Ostler' (a slighting reference to his position as Elizabeth's Master of Horse).

Page 24. *Netherlanders.* The Protestant rebels against Spanish rule received discreet help from England, but Elizabeth did not openly approve of rebels. These negotiations for a marriage have nothing to do with love, and probably Elizabeth had no intention of allowing them to succeed.

Page 27. *To Nonsuch, then.* These moves from one royal palace to another need not be accompanied by any change of scene. They are devices to indicate lapses of time, during which Cecil and Dudley talk things over apart.

Page 28. *messenger from Scotland.* Much of this dialogue with Davison is based on records of a conversation with a Scots envoy, James Melville. But there the situation is reversed: instead of a young Englishman annoying Elizabeth by his admiration for Mary, Melville was a Scotsman delighting her by his flattery. He tried to dodge some of her teasing questions inviting comparison between the two queens, but the final score in this playful game placed Elizabeth above Mary. This modified version of the interview has advantages: it introduces the important fact about Mary that men fell under the spell of her charms; it shows us something of Elizabeth's way with men—now playful, now tyrannical, vain, demanding flattery, and yet realistic; and as the conversation runs, it brings up the scheme of marrying Dudley to Mary. This leads to the spectacle of Elizabeth sacrificing her feelings as a woman to accept, as a politician, Cecil's crafty scheme, because she can see its advantages for the country.

The introduction of Davison here, as the susceptible young envoy to Mary, provides a grimly ironic touch at the end, when he is the bearer of the warrant for her execution.

Page 31. *A conspiracy.* Only one of many, mostly originating in the North, smelt out by Walsingham over a period of 20 years. Walsingham organised a cunning and ruthless spy system.

Do as we command. An economical way of showing that although Elizabeth might vacillate, she would stand no insubordination when her mind was made up. Contrast Mary's trouble with Knox.

Cecil, you are very welcome. This dialogue with Cecil concentrates in a few dramatic moments the exchanges of several months. The idea of a marriage to Darnley was no sudden shock to Cecil or Elizabeth. At the court ceremony when Dudley was created Earl of Leicester (in order to make him more eligible for Mary), Elizabeth turned to Melville (the Scots envoy) and asked him how he liked him, then teasingly suggested that he preferred 'yon long lad', pointing to Darnley. Melville diplomatically answered that no woman

of spirit could prefer Darnley. Later Elizabeth refused to allow
Darnley to go to Scotland, but in February 1565 she agreed (at
Cecil's suggestion) to let him go. At the same time she made Mary
an offer: if she would marry Leicester (Dudley) he would be
advanced to the highest possible honours and Elizabeth would
support Mary's claim to the English succession. Mary was insulted.

Why should Elizabeth object to Darnley as a husband for Mary?
He was less dangerous than a European prince such as Don Carlos.
He was a Catholic, but not a very powerful or devoted one. He
might even have turned Protestant if enough inducement had
been offered. The real danger was in the powerful claim to the
throne of England presented by a union of Mary and Darnley,
both descended directly from Henry VII. Henry's daughter
Margaret Tudor had married first James IV of Scotland (Mary's
grandfather) and afterwards the Scots Earl of Angus, Darnley's
grandfather. A son of Mary and Darnley would have an unbeatable
claim to the throne of England—which, in fact, he did inherit,
on the death of Elizabeth. Even so, Elizabeth could possibly have
been won over. She had a right to be consulted, since Darnley was
her subject. Instead, Mary and Darnley behaved defiantly. When
Darnley was commanded to return to England, his reply was to
marry the Scots queen. Elizabeth supported with money the
rebellion against the marriage, but it failed. Mary was triumphant.

But the marriage was a blunder. She had made the mistake of
falling in love with Darnley (who was tall, fair, athletic, a good
lute player) and letting love determine her policy. Within three
months she knew him for a dissolute, unreliable, arrogant weak-
ling.

Page 38. *Do you pay court in Edinburgh?* Not an altogether impossible
result. Later, when Mary was a prisoner in England, Cecil took
care to be courteous to her, just in case he was dealing with a future
Queen of England. Later he sent his son back and forth to the
young James, which greatly displeased Elizabeth.

Page 40. *Half Italian.* There was widespread malicious gossip about the
paternity of the expected child, who was sometimes later referred
to as 'Davie's son'. Morton was conspicuous among the trouble-
makers, insinuating that Rizzio was Mary's lover. Nobody knows
whether he was, but the child was almost certainly Darnley's.

Page 43. *fascinated by your rough provincial masculinity.* Mary is sarcastic, but what she says is partly true, as Bothwell knows. The whole of this scene of political and sexual fencing expresses the mingled attraction and repulsion in her reaction to him, summed up in his parting words: 'I was goin'—you keep stoppin' me.'

Page 44. *Letter to Rome.* Mary's allies are deserting her; she turns to Bothwell for support, but his terms are unacceptable; she is not yet ready to succumb to his bold wooing style and his assumption that he would be the dominant partner. So she asked for help from Pope Pius V. He was willing to send money to pay troops, but she was hesitant to fall in with the Pope's intentions by suppressing Protestantism.

Page 47. *Suppose he was King.* The Protestant lords despise Darnley, but are now plotting to make him a puppet-king in order to upset Mary's authority. These unlikely allies were united in jealousy and hatred of Rizzio. He had once been Darnley's bosom friend, but as Darnley declined in Mary's favour, Rizzio advanced, until his wealth, power and arrogance were offensive to everybody at court.

Page 49. *A wee paper.* An example of what Robert Bolt has called 'simplifying but not falsifying' history for the purposes of the play. There were actually two bonds, both committing the signatories to granting the Crown Matrimonial to Darnley and upholding the Protestant religion in Scotland. Only one of them mentioned the murder of Rizzio (and that obscurely). It was signed by Morton, Ruthven and Lindsey (both of whom were married into Morton's family) and others. Darnley did not actually sign this, but they took care to implicate him fully. Mary always believed, probably rightly, that the full intention was to kill her and her unborn child at the same time. Time is telescoped here, and the confused happenings have been organised to make a clear and well-shaped scene. Our knowledge of what actually happened depends on the eye-witness accounts of two deeply-interested parties—Ruthven and Mary herself. They did not tell quite the same tale.

The murderers did not surprise Rizzio alone with the queen, as in the play: they burst in on a supper-party, with Lady Argyll and attendants also present. It was not Morton, but his bastard brother, who stabbed Rizzio with Darnley's dagger. It is a fine piece of drama to have Darnley's dagger handed back to him across the stage, so that his implication in the murder is manifest to all; but this could not have been done by Bothwell. He had escaped out of a window, having guessed that the conspirators meant to murder him too, and was on his way to Dunbar. To Dunbar Mary eventually made her way, but not so directly as in the play. There was first a night and day of mingled horror, grief, anger, and cold resolve on revenge, in which Mary showed great courage and cunning. She battered the frightened Darnley with contempt until he was ready to listen to her persuasion; she convinced him that his new friends and fellow-conspirators were his enemies; finally she induced him to desert them and to help her to escape. Two nights after the murder they got away together from Holyrood and rode to join Bothwell at Dunbar. Bothwell raised 8,000 men, and only nine days after the murder Mary rode into Edinburgh at the head of her army. Morton, Ruthven and Lindsay fled to England.

Mary wrote a full account to her dear cousin in England. At the beginning of Act II (page 54) Elizabeth muses admiringly and enviously on Mary's resourceful and adventurous triumph over her troubles. Later Mary pardoned the murderers, but it is unlikely that she forgave any of them, least of all her husband. The complete story makes an exciting narrative, but it does not fit without selection and adjustment into an effective stage-play.

ACT II

Page 53. *font*. Although Elizabeth had never officially countenanced the marriage to Darnley, she agreed to be a godmother (absentee) to the child, and sent a gold font as a present. A more remarkable absentee from the ceremony was the father. Darnley had objected, in vain, to the invitation to Elizabeth; he may have sulked because his protest was overridden. Robert Bolt has pointed out that Darnley's nose was also out of joint because of Mary's flagrant association with Bothwell. Or was he ill with syphilis?

Royal Warrant. Elizabeth is not the only one in this play who attached importance to a royal warrant for killing. She felt a human distaste for execution, yet could not openly condone lawlessness.

Page 54. *we aid no rebels*. Similarly she was furtive in her aid of rebels, either in Scotland or the Netherlands, and always ready to repudiate them if challenged. She said this to Moray but gave him a little money. Robert Bolt comments: 'She is a master of political expediency. She loathes aiding rebels, but she has no political principle. In short she sees that to be a great queen she must be an unnatural monster. She would have been happier if she had been less intelligent.'

she escapes. Elizabeth envies Mary her involvement in life, with all its dangers and hardships. By contrast her own existence seems a barren avoidance of life, a sacrifice to the interests of the State.

Page 55. *She ascends to throne*. Elizabeth sits on her throne at Whitehall while the christening ceremony takes place downstage at Stirling Castle.

what manner of reply you gave. Mary's ironical reply shows how little she trusts the apparent friendliness of Elizabeth. The inclusion of England in the child's titles is hardly placatory. As the author has commented: 'She has the bit between her teeth here, triumphant as woman and queen, it seems, with a dashing lover, a boy child, an heir to England.'

Lord Protector. Mary has earlier (page 43) offered this honour and responsibility to Bothwell: now she thinks better of it. In fact, the Earls of Mar were hereditary Protectors of the royal heirs of Scotland.

Page 56. *being your slave*. Mary's infatuation with Darnley was a disastrous mistake; her submission to Bothwell a calamitous blunder. Just when and how far she succumbed to his 'rough provincial masculinity' is disputed, but he had always attracted her as a strong man whom she might turn to in trouble, and she had no doubt remembered that he had supported her mother Mary of Guise, and believed that he had saved not only her own throne but her life itself after the murder of Rizzio. She probably fell in love while nursing him from a serious wound contracted in one of his endless forays on the border from Dunbar.

Page 57. *I'll fetch him*. If she did not suspect that Bothwell intended to murder Darnley, what did she think was the purpose of luring him from his safe retreat in Glasgow? He was ill, but why should she (much less Bothwell) bring him to Edinburgh for treatment? A likely explanation is that he was intriguing against her, and she thought he would be less dangerous in Edinburgh, away from his friends and relations. (The author has commented that she was morally ambiguous, and hiding from herself what she did not want to know.)

powder. Gunpowder was used on this occasion, rather than the more usual weapon—the dagger—in the hope of hiding all traces. In the event the guilt was never conclusively fixed, though several people were later executed for their part.

Page 58. *a letter.* Bothwell here reads out fragments from the second of the Casket Letters, which, if genuine, would be damning evidence of Mary's complicity in the murder of her husband. It may be wholly a forgery, or perhaps a genuine love letter from Mary with interpolations from a letter to Bothwell from another woman. It runs to 3,500 words. The Casket, containing letters, poems and documents, was allegedly found among Bothwell's papers after the confrontation at Carberry Hill (see note on p. 62). It was produced at a time convenient for Mary's accusers. The extant documents are clerk's copies of the originals, which mysteriously disappeared soon after they had been examined by an English commission appointed by Elizabeth to investigate the evidence against Mary. When Elizabeth had seen their report she pronounced: 'There has been nothing produced nor shewn against the Queen their sovereign whereby the Queen of England should conceive or take any evil opinion of the Queen her good sister for anything yet seen.' (But Mary was at this time imprisoned in England, and Elizabeth did not release her.)

Robert Bolt leaves his audience in no doubt that Mary wrote a love letter to Bothwell from Glasgow, where she was visiting Darnley. It seems that Bothwell is not interested in the love messages—only in whether Darnley is coming. He keeps the letter as his 'warrant' for the murder. Yet Mary is left in ignorance of Bothwell's plan, and she is troubled by pity for Darnley, and even a wish to protect him.

Page 59. *the castle.* Darnley himself declined to enter Craigmillar Castle, and preferred Kirk o' Field, a house just inside the wall of Edinburgh. He actually stayed a week there, frequently visited by Mary. Their supposed reconciliation recalls another one after the murder of Rizzio, and may have been as deceptive. Mary appeared attentive, and Darnley rather fretful.

humorous. Damp

Page 60. *Bastien.* Bastien Pages was a favourite page, whose wedding took place on the morning of February 9th, attended by the Queen. It was celebrated by a masque that evening, which she promised to attend. But she had also promised Darnley that she would spend the night at Kirk o' Field. In the end she went to the masque and (fortunately) did not return to Kirk o' Field. In this scene Bothwell's ambiguous reference to Bastien is meant to warn her that her own prospects of marrying him depend on her choosing Holyrood.

do not know. Evidently Mary knew what was in the wind, but was enabled by Bothwell to avoid facing it.

pavane. A pavane is a stately dance, here intended to become symbolic, a spell-bound movement under Bothwell's hypnotic influence.

Mary, Mary, quite contrary. This nursery rhyme is said to have referred to Mary Stuart. If so, the bells may suggest the sanctus, the cockle shells may refer to pilgrims and the pretty maids may be the four Maries who attended the queen. An apparently innocent inquiry (in a child's voice) about the state of the realm under this Catholic Queen (or the garden may be her soul) is full of irony at this moment when she is abandoning the moral teaching of her Church. But the purpose of the lines is suggestion, not explicit admonition.

Page 61. *distant explosion*. The explosion at 2.00 a.m. on February 10th at Kirk o' Field, nearly a mile from Holyrood, wrecked the house, but did not kill Darnley, who was found strangled in the garden, nobody knows by whom. Robert Bolt deals with the murder and its unsolved mysteries in one off-stage bang, and moves on to its repercussions in Europe. All Mary's contemporaries reckoned Bothwell was responsible, and most historians have agreed.

Bring him to trial. Elizabeth wrote at length to Mary urging this course. Mary appeared to be paralysed by shock, and sank into one of her periodical bouts of illness. She would not or could not or dared not arraign Bothwell. Following the practice of the times, she should have arrested and brought to trial *somebody* who could be made to carry the blame for the time being. Two months later she gave formal permission for Bothwell to be brought to trial, but in a private process initiated by Darnley's father, Lennox.

the manner of the trial. Bothwell arrived at the court accompanied by a strong force of his own men. Lennox set out with an equivalent force, but was intercepted and forbidden to enter the city with more than six followers. He therefore refused to appear. Morton excused himself from service on the jury on the grounds that he was a kinsman of the victim. Bothwell so terrorized the Court that not a single witness for the prosecution appeared! Not surprisingly, he was acquitted. After the trial he offered to fight anybody who doubted his innocence. Nobody accepted the challenge, though doubt was widespread.

we are married. A week after the trial, Bothwell induced eight bishops and fifteen nobles (including Morton) to sign a bond re-affirming his innocence and promising to support his marriage to the Queen if she should choose him as husband. He then abducted Mary by a show of force—though she offered no resistance—and married her three weeks later.

a Protestant pantomime. For two reasons Catholics could not accept the marriage as valid: Bothwell was already married until only twelve days before, when he had managed to arrange a divorce; and the royal wedding at Holyrood was celebrated according to Protestant rites.

Page 62. *involved against her will.* This seemed to many the only explanation, though Mary never confirmed it. Ironically, the supposition was used by Morton and his followers to repudiate the bond they had signed in favour of the marriage. (But Morton didn't believe it himself.) They now mobilised against Mary and Bothwell.

Let us have Bothwell. The brief scene presents in theatrical terms the confrontation of the two armies at Carberry Hill, near Edinburgh, on June 15th, 1567. Morton led the Protestant lords, including Mar, Lindsay and Ruthven: a smaller army was commanded by Bothwell with Mary at his side. Mary at first refused to abandon her husband, who then offered to fight a champion, preferably Morton. Morton declined and offered the role to Lindsay; but while preparations for the combat were going on, the royal troops were melting away. The Lords were winning without fighting. Mary then agreed to surrender if they would let Bothwell go. After a moving farewell before the whole array, Bothwell galloped away to Dunbar. They never saw each other again, though in the coming weeks Bothwell made strenuous efforts to help her.

Mary was taken, a humiliated prisoner, weeping and mud-spattered, through the streets of Edinburgh, where people shouted insults and threats.

Ormiston. He had been Bothwell's henchman in the Kirk o' Field
murder. In fact they didn't catch him and hang him till some years
later. The claim that he has already been hanged is really an
indication that the Lords will be ruthless. As stage dialogue it is
much more effective than a prophecy that they will hang him at
some date in the future. It also indicates that Bothwell's position is
more desperate than he had realised.

A Hepburn! A clan rallying cry. Bothwell was James Hepburn, Earl of
Bothwell. But nobody comes to his aid. This is a dramatic repre-
sentation of the melting away of his forces at Carberry Hill.

Page 64. put him to the horn. Outlaw him. He did come back and they did
put him to the horn. He escaped to Shetland.

'I would follow him . . .'. The author points out that this declaration by
Mary was accepted by contemporaries as her actual words and
certainly expressed her attitude at this point. The relationship had
deteriorated until the disaster overtook them, and then all Mary's
romanticism came out.

the keep on an island. The castle of Sir William Douglas, a cousin of
Morton, was on an island on Loch Leven in Kinross-shire. There
she was kept in harsh, humiliating confinement for ten months,
during which she was forced under threats of death to abdicate,
and appoint her half-brother Moray as Regent. The story of her
betrayal, ill-treatment and her romantic escape, followed by the
mustering of an army (within a few days nine earls and nine
bishops had declared for her) of about 6,000 supporters and her
disastrous defeat and flight to England—all this is managed in a
page of dialogue. The temptation to dwell on exciting or romantic
or poignant incidents has been resisted where they are not clearly
relevant to the main theme, the sacrifices made for power in the
interweaving careers of Mary and Elizabeth. Such matters as
Mary's ability to evoke romantic devotion in young men like the
young Douglas of Loch Leven, or the reasons for her irrevocable
blunder in fleeing to England rather than to France, however
fascinating to the student of Mary Queen of Scots, can be noted
only in passing.

Page 65. Who has the child? A question of vital importance. Elizabeth
would have liked to have him brought up in England. In fact he was
still in the hands of the Earl of Mar. George Buchanan became his

tutor from the age of four, and taught him to hate his mother as a murderer and adultress. The child was crowned James VI of Scotland at the age of 13 months. The essential point Bolt expresses is that James was brought up by Presbyterian divines.

Rule Scotland wisely. Moray was Regent of Scotland until his assassination in 1570. Morton became Regent the following year. Elizabeth did not openly recognise the forced abdication of Mary and the proclamation of Moray as Regent, but she liked to keep her options open. She was kept informed of all that happened in Scotland. Mary had written to her from her prison in Loch Leven, concluding 'Ayez pitié de votre bonne soeur et cousine.'

Page 66. *Why me?* A reasonable query. In France Mary would have been among friends and relations. She must sometimes have thought of Elizabeth as her friend, not her enemy. She genuinely expected Elizabeth to help her regain the throne of Scotland.

a Trojan Horse. She was an unwelcome present—a rallying-point inside England for its enemies.

She's yours. Her arrival was a real problem. The Scots did not want her back. Elizabeth didn't want her, but didn't want to help her to France or Scotland. Mary continually hoped to be received at Court, but Elizabeth said she could not receive her until she had been cleared of guilt for Darnley's murder. It suited Elizabeth to leave the matter unsettled; meanwhile Mary was a permanent source of danger.

a letter. This is again the Long Letter brought to Bothwell (see p. 58).

Page 67. *that is no forgery.* Elizabeth's intuition tells her that it is a genuine love letter.

Sheffield Castle. Only one of the several castles—Bolton in Wensleydale, Tutbury, Chartley, Fotheringay and others—in which Mary spent her 19 years of imprisonment.

Page 68. *our Queen sees Mary in the mirror.* Partly the point of the play. The resemblances in situation are as interesting as the differences in temperament. The scandal following the murder of Darnley resembles that associated with the death of Amy Robsart. Elizabeth knew what it was like to be Mary.

Lord Shrewsbury. He *was* a kindly jailer. Her household was supposed to be limited to 30, but he let it creep up to 41, including servants attending on attendants. At one time she had 10 horses, and went not merely riding but hunting. He was £10,000 a year out of pocket on the cost of keeping his prisoner in the royal style she expected. The supply of beer has a more sinister significance later, under a severer regime.

My Lord Bothwell. After his expulsion from Scotland he became a pirate operating from Shetland, until he was driven out. In Norway he resumed brief contact with a former mistress, but Mary had no reason to speak so bitterly of him. She herself was carrying on a tender correspondence with a man she was hoping to marry—the Duke of Norfolk, and therefore exploring the possibilities of a divorce from Bothwell. He is said to have agreed to this. If there ever was a passionate love between them, it had burnt out; but relations remained amicable. From Norway Bothwell went on to Denmark, where he spent the last eleven years of his life in a succession of prisons, each more rigorous than the last. His fate was more horrible than Mary's; he died insane, chained to a pillar in a dungeon where there was no room to stand, in 1578.

Page 69. *the little man in Scotland.* She sent Nau on a mission to her little boy, but he was not allowed to see him or to pass on her messages.

Page 70. *policy.* Statecraft: Nau's modern use of the word is a kind of pun.

this gentleman whom I met. This is the first reference to a series of plots being hatched around her during her imprisonment. At the beginning she was too shrewd to encourage plans which offered little chance of success, and her aim continued to be to avoid giving anybody evidence that she was implicated. J. E. Neale says (in *Queen Elizabeth*): 'Time and again when talking to English officials, she called God to witness and vowed her most solemn oath that she knew of no conspiracy against Elizabeth, nor would consent to any, but her soul was no sooner forsworn than she was writing to conspirators to launch the invasion without thought of peril to her.'

if we live it not at all. Living a full life meant for her being a queen. The scene cuts to cries of a man being tortured for his efforts to restore her to the full life.

Page 71. *Regnans in Excelsis.* This Papal bull (1570) gravely changed the situation in a way that Mary had not sought. It made all Catholic missionaries in England liable to be arraigned as traitors, since treason was from now on a duty.

Page 72. *Fenton.* Fenton and the manner of his trapping are an invention but very typical of many individuals and Walsingham's unpleasant but effective methods.

   Douai. A Catholic seminary in the Netherlands, founded in 1568 to educate English priests to work for the Counter-Reformation in England.

   an instrument of Master Walsingham's. Walsingham was highly successful in placing his agents at the very centre of conspiracies against Elizabeth.

Page 73. *Spanish armies in the Netherlands.* They were occupied in trying to suppress Protestant rebels, but they were a potential threat to England.

Page 74. *Earl of Leicester.* He had secretly married the Countess of Essex. Although the long-standing affair between Elizabeth and Leicester had cooled to a sentimental friendship, Elizabeth was angry, all the more so because he had opposed her marriage to the Duke of Alençon. Leicester knew the Queen would be insanely jealous, so much so that he kept it a secret from her and no one else dared tell her, with the result that when she did find out her first impulse was to put him in the Tower. For a long time she would not speak to or recognise his wife.

Page 76. *The French Alliance.* Elizabeth had carried on a lively flirtation with the Duke of Alençon, brother and heir to Henry III of France. He was 20 years younger (she was now 45), ugly but attractive. Though a Catholic, he had fought for the Huguenots in France and the Protestant rebels in the Netherlands. In England the Council were divided, but the people were said to be strongly against the marriage. Elizabeth had a political interest in keeping the prospect dangling: she kept the Netherlands troublesome to Spain, and kept open the option of a firm alliance with France. Did she ever mean to marry him? If not, why not? Nobody knows.

   100,000 crowns. In June, 1581, she sent him £30,000 to help finance his activities in the Netherlands, but it was not enough. He came to see her and was promised more, on conditions most favourable to England. Walking in a gallery at Whitehall, with the French Ambassador and others in attendance, she kissed him and told him she would marry him. She also promised him more money. She was still keeping up the courtship (but with fading ardour) when he died of a fever in June, 1584.

Page 79. *dossiers*. The piling up of dossiers in the unwilling hands of the
Spanish Ambassador is a device for impressing on the audience,
visually and very dramatically, the accumulated evidence of plots
against the queen's life, spreading over a period of sixteen years.
The names are those of conspirators, some of them double agents
working for Walsingham's secret service. Ridolfi tried to organise
an invasion of England by Spanish troops from the Netherlands,
coinciding with a Catholic rising in England. The intention was to
place Mary on the English throne, with the Duke of Norfolk. Norfolk was executed in June, 1572. Throgmorton led the first of three
major conspiracies in the 1580s. Creighton was involved in a
widespread conspiracy called the Enterprise. In the play, as in
historical fact, these conspiracies culminated in the Babington
Plot, which made Mary's execution inevitable. She had denied
knowledge of the previous ones, but this time she could not.
Sir Anthony Babington wrote to her on July 6th, 1586, telling her
what was proposed. Nau advised her to leave the letter unanswered,
but she replied giving approval. So she fell into a trap carefully
laid for her.

The confrontation with the Spanish Ambassador in the play
is immensely effective, and shaped to a climax which was less
perfectly timed in reality. The ambassador (Mendoza—de Quadra
had died long before this) was summoned to court at the discovery
of the Throgmorton Plot. He was expelled (and not replaced)
in 1583. But he was deeply involved in the Babington Plot from a
safe retreat in Paris. It was there that he received his letters from
Babington.

Page 80. *proof pedantic*. Proof sufficient to convince the most meticulous.
a very calculating boy. James was now 20, and described as 'a very old
young man'. He made a cautious show of concern for the ex-Queen
of Scotland, but was more interested in his own prospects as a
future King of England.

Page 81. *a freak in nature*. She was already 54, well past normal child-
bearing age. (But at the time of the Alençon marriage proposal
the French ambassador had told of a neighbour of his—an
Englishwoman who was pregnant at 56!)

she thinks him loyal and loving. She did, and she trusted his ambassador
until she found they were both playing her false (see below).

Page 85. *no visitors*. Walsingham is here represented as coming in person to impose restrictions on Mary. They were actually imposed on her by a newly appointed custodian, Sir Amyas Paulet, at the grim castle of Tutbury. Although fictional, the incident does express in a distilled form the reality of what was happening— Walsingham steadily increasing the rigours of her imprisonment and Mary building a sentimental and unjustified expectation on James and flying to mad imprudence when she finally understands that he is indifferent. The cloth of state ('that thing') was very important to her; it was not taken down until she had been tried and found guilty.

Page 87. *Child's toys*. It is true that the presents she had sent to her son had all been stopped. Here the discovery of what Elizabeth's agents have done to destroy the mother/child relationship is a *coup de theatre*, a bitter shock that goads her into the reckless decision to support the Babington Plot. She was indeed goaded into reck-lessness by news about her son, but it was the revelation that he had signed a treaty of alliance with Elizabeth, ignoring her interests.

practice. Treachery

Page 88. *brewer*. This man (nicknamed 'the honest man') worked at first in good faith for Mary, but later received pay from Gifford and Walsingham as well as Mary, and had the cheek to demand a higher price for his beer! (It is now January 1586.)

Page 89. *warrant for her execution*. The author foregoes the dramatic scope in the trial, in which Mary defended herself with dignity and eloquence, but moves on to the problem raised for Elizabeth by the verdict of guilty. By now the demand for her death was widespread and powerful, but Elizabeth wanted to avoid respon-sibility for it.

Nothing from Scotland. James had earlier appealed for her life, and after her death he was moved by the indignation in Scotland to break off formal relations (for a time), but at this stage he was canny. 'Master James was still first and foremost interested in Master James', says J. E. Neale, who reports that he wrote to Leicester: 'How fond and inconstant I were if I should prefer my mother to the title, let all men judge'.

Sheffield. The trial and execution were actually at Fotheringay, Northants.

Davison. He had recently been appointed second secretary under

Walsingham. Elizabeth used him as the scapegoat she wanted. She first suggested that Sir Amyas Paulet should 'shorten the life' of his prisoner, but he replied 'God forbid that I should make so foul a shipwreck of my conscience, to shed blood without law or warrant.' So the warrant was sent and carried out; then she said she had never meant to send it. Davison was imprisoned in the Tower for 18 months. He was released after the defeat of the Armada had made Elizabeth more secure, and he continued to be paid as secretary.

Page 91. *life that is avoided.* This is an interpretation of her motives and points the contrast with Elizabeth. Elizabeth did not exactly avoid life, but cautiously denied herself the passion of her impetuous cousin.

words for saying what she was not. Cecil lists the qualities that make Elizabeth a great queen, but her closing words question the ultimate satisfaction of that.

Page 92. *Triumphant fanfare.* The irony of Elizabeth's disillusioned words is pointed by the fanfare and the cries of '*Vivat Regina*'—'Long live the queen'. At this point we may remember the author's theme—'the impermissible sacrifice of self which Power demands, and gets, and squanders—to what purpose ?''. As a queen, she has triumphed: as a woman, she is a frightening figure even to herself.